KU-570-484

The Fast-Track MBA Series

Co-published with AMED (the Association for Management Education and Development)

Consultant Editors
John Kind, Director, Harbridge Consulting Group
David Megginson, Associate Head, Sheffield Business School

THE FAST-TRACK MBA SERIES represents an innovative and refreshingly different approach to presenting core subjects in a typical MBA syllabus in a lively and accessible way. The usual text book approach is eschewed in favour of a practical, action-oriented style which involves the reader in self-assessment and participation.

Ideal for managers wanting to renew or develop their management capabilities, the books in THE FAST-TRACK MBA SERIES rapidly give readers a sound knowledge of all aspects of business and management that will boost both self-confidence and career prospects. For those fortunate enough to take an MBA, the Series will provide a solid grounding in the subjects to be studied. Managers and students worldwide will find this new series an exciting and challenging alternative to the usual study texts and management guides.

Titles already available in the series are:

★ *Strategic Management* (Robert Grant & James Craig)
★ *Organisational Behaviour and Design* (Barry Cushway & Derek Lodge)
★ *Problem Solving and Decision Making* (Graham Wilson)
★ *Human Resource Development* (David Megginson, Jennifer Joy-Matthews & Paul Banfield)
★ *Accounting for Managers* (Graham Mott)

Forthcoming books in the series will cover:

Data Analysis and IT ★ Financial Management ★ International Management ★ Investment and Risk ★ Law ★ Business Ethics ★ Economics ★ Marketing ★ Operations Management.

AMED is an association of individuals who have a professional interest in the development of people at work. AMED's network brings together people from industry, the public sector, academic organizations and consultancy, and is exclusive to individuals.

The aims of AMED are to promote best practice in the fields of individual and organizational development, to provide a forum for the exploration of new ideas, to offer members opportunities for their own development and to encourage the adoption of ethical practices in development.

For further information on AMED you are invited to write to AMED, 21 Catherine Street, London WC2B 5JS.

The Series Editors

John Kind is a director of Harbridge House, a consultancy firm specializing in management development and training. He has wide experience of designing and presenting business education programmes in various parts of the world for clients such as BAA, Bass, British Petroleum and General Electric. John Kind is a visiting lecturer at Henley Management College and holds an MBA from the Manchester Business School and an honours degree in Economics.

David Megginson is a writer and researcher on self-development and the line manager as developer. He has written *A Manager's Guide to Coaching, Self-development: A Facilitator's Guide, Human Resource Development* in the Fast-track MBA series, *The Line Managers as Developer* and the *Developing the Developers* research report. He consults and researches in blue chip companies, and public and voluntary organizations. He is a director of the European Mentoring Centre and an elected Council member of AMED, and has been Associate Head of Sheffield Business School and a National Assessor for the National Training Awards.

Sally Yeung, Partner, Lansdell Associates, is a freelance writer, editor and translator. Previously director of the Association for Management Education and Development and Research Associate at Ashridge Strategic Management Centre, she is the author of books and articles on mission and corporate philosophy, organization development, managing change and Japanese management.

Human Resource Management

BARRY CUSHWAY

Published in association with AMED

KOGAN
PAGE

First published in 1994

Apart from any fair dealing for the purposes of research or private study, or criticism or review, as permitted under the Copyright, Designs and Patents Act, 1988, this publication may only be reproduced, stored or transmitted, in any form or by any means, with the prior permission in writing of the publishers, or in the case of reprographic reproduction in accordance with the terms of licences issued by the Copyright Licensing Agency. Enquiries concerning reproduction outside those terms should be sent to the publishers at the undermentioned address:

Kogan Page Limited
120 Pentonville Road
London N1 9JN
© Barry Cushway, 1994

British Library Cataloguing in Publication Data

A CIP record for this book is available from the British Library.

ISBN 0 7494 1172 4

Typeset by DP Photosetting, Aylesbury, Bucks
Printed in England by
Clays Ltd, St Ives plc

Contents

6   Contents

Acknowledgements

I would like to acknowledge the assistance and support I have received and needed from so many different sources. In particular I would like to thank Bob Edenborough, Richard Knowles and Doug Alexander at MSL for helpful comments on various chapters, Dave Speller at the London Borough of Bexley, Mary Pierson at Wellcome and Vivienne Hole for more information on performance management than I could possibly use. I have particularly welcomed the encouraging noises made by Philip Mudd at Kogan Page, as I needed all the encouragement I could get. I would like to thank my wife for tolerating my hours of incarceration slaving over a hot word processor and for keeping the tea coming. I would also like to thank the reviewer for his perceptive comments.

managing people has become more complex, partly because of recent employment legislation, and partly because of the recognition that a strategic approach has to be taken to the management of the organization's most important resource. As organizations have grown in size and complexity, and as the pace of change has increased, it has been recognized that organization-wide strategies and processes have to be developed to assist managers and that this requires a dedicated human resource function.

The precise origins of what we would understand by human resource management can be debated. It could be argued that it originated the first time any group of people were organized to achieve a common purpose. No doubt Roman legions had problems of managing motivation and morale, promotions, training, discipline, pay, health, etc. In terms of modern human resource management, at least in the UK, the beginning of the professional function is generally viewed as the pre-World War II welfare officer. In the 1950s and 1960s personnel managers began to be appointed, and establishment officers in the public sector. Their main role was often as a kind of gatekeeper. They would ensure that all the correct procedures were followed and that employment contracts and other legal documents were issued, maintain personnel records, negotiate with the trade unions and advise on disciplinary matters. The role was primarily a reactive one concerned with maintaining systems.

Not only has the burgeoning volume of legislation in the last few decades increased the need for highly knowledgeable personnel professionals to be able to advise managers and to implement procedures, but so has the increased recognition of the importance of people for organizational success. Much of the credit for this recognition should go to the human relations movement which drew attention to the importance of people to the organization — something which seems to have rather been taken for granted or not recognized up to then. Perhaps people were regarded as a resource but it was an expendable one, as World War I depressingly illustrated. Similarly the growth in the recognition of individual rights in the workplace has led to greater emphasis on developing systems and procedures that meet individuals' needs and expectations, not just those of the organization.

The net effect of all of this is that the human resource function has grown and developed to such an extent that it is commonly thought of as having usurped the function of the line manager. With the general movement towards empowerment of employees, this has meant that there has recently been an increased emphasis on delegating human resource responsibilities to line managers rather than relying totally on a central function.

DEFINITION OF HUMAN RESOURCE MANAGEMENT

Human resource management is therefore part of the process that helps the organization achieve its objectives. Once the general direction and strategy have been established the next stage is to formulate firm objectives and develop these into action plans. The objectives cannot be attained without the required resources, which of course includes people. HRM should be part of the process which determines what people are required, how to use them, how to get them and how to manage them. It should be fully integrated with all the other management processes.

The place of HRM in relation to the organization's other activities is summarized in Figure 1.1.

Torrington and Hall[2] define personnel management as:

> a series of activities which: first enable working people and their employing organizations to agree about the objectives and nature of their working relationship and, secondly, ensures that the agreement is fulfilled.

This definition stresses the mutual nature of the employment relationship and emphasizes that it is only by reciprocity that both the individual and the organization are likely to achieve their objectives.

Taking the above definition as a starting point human resource management can be defined as:

> a range of strategies, processes and activities designed to support

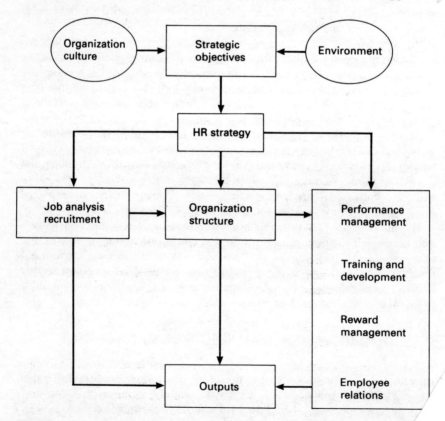

Figure 1.1 *The human resource management process*

corporate objectives by integrating the needs of the organization and the individuals that comprise it.

In this definition more emphasis is placed on the strategic importance of HRM and on processes, because of the continuous nature of the activities carried out. While there is less emphasis on the need for agreement, because it is a fact that some personnel policies are, and perhaps have to be, implemented as a purely managerial exercise, the importance of integrating the two sets of needs is underlined.

OBJECTIVES OF HRM

The precise objectives of human resource management will vary from organization to organization and will depend on the organization's stage of development. At one extreme, for example, the human resource specialist will be seen as someone who looks after the administrative side of people management, ie preparing contracts of employment, maintaining personnel files and so on. At the other extreme he or she will be seen as an integral and vital part of the business planning process. The objectives of HRM, therefore, are many and various and will at different times include some, if not all, of the following:

- Advising management on the human resource policies required to ensure that the organization has a highly motivated and high-performing workforce, has people equipped to cope with change and meets its legal employment obligations.
- Implementing and maintaining all necessary human resource policies and procedures to enable the organization to achieve its objectives.
- Assisting in the development of the organization's overall direction and strategy, particularly with regard to the human resource implications.
- Providing the support and conditions that will help line managers achieve their objectives.
- Handling crises and difficult human relations situations to ensure that they do not get in the way of the organization achieving its objectives.
- Providing a communications link between the workforce and the organization's management.
- Acting as a custodian of organizational standards and values in the management of human resources.

MAIN HRM ACTIVITIES

The main activities which make up the personnel function can be considered in terms of those that apply before, during and after the appointment of employees. To put it another way, HRM relates to the acquisition, management and disposal of resources which in this case happen to consist of people.

Resource acquisition

The first step in the process involves establishing the organization's requirement for the resource in question, in terms of quantity, type and quality. In particular it entails:

- Advising on the kind of organization structure required to deliver the strategy, ie how activities should be grouped together, who should report to whom, how decisions should be made and communicated, etc.
- Planning and advising on the number, levels and types of jobs required for the organization to meet its objectives in the most cost-effective way, including the extent to which activities should be resourced from outside the organization.
- Designing jobs in terms of duties and responsibilities, reporting lines and supervisory role.
- Advising on the most effective way of acquiring the people required.
- Managing or advising on the selection process to ensure that the applicants selected have the skills, knowledge and experience necessary to be able to carry out the duties required to the appropriate standard, and that the process is carried out equitably and is free from bias against minority groups.

Resource management

Once the organization has all the people it requires to achieve its objectives, the next priority should be to ensure that those people remain with the organization long enough to be effective and that they perform well while they are there. This involves the following:

- Designing performance management processes that will help people know what is expected of them and to increase the possibility that they will achieve their identified objectives — although it is essential that any such process is owned and managed by the line managers.
- Designing and running training programmes to ensure that employees have the necessary knowledge, skills and approach to carry out their responsibilities effectively.
- Designing and running development programmes to equip employees to undertake more responsible jobs and to assist in career management and succession planning.
- Advising on and administering reward strategies that support the organization's objectives and business plan and which provide a level of remuneration sufficient to attract and retain employees of the right calibre.
- Consulting and negotiating with trade unions and employee representatives on terms and conditions of employment.
- Advising on the administration of disciplinary and grievance issues.
- Advising on the most effective means of communicating with employees and of involving them in the organization's decision-making processes.

■ Advising on staff changes, eg in terms of revised duties, relocation, transfers of undertakings, etc.
■ Advising on staff welfare and health and safety issues.
■ Maintaining all necessary administrative and legal processes connected with employment, such as contracts of employment, personnel records and personal files, etc.
■ Formulating and recommending employment policies on issues such as equal opportunities, smoking at work, harassment, etc.
■ Advising line managers on all employment policies and on employment law and ensuring that the organization meets legal and social obligations.

Resource disposal

There always comes a point at which the organization and the employee have to part company. The reason might be retirement, resignation, expiry of a fixed-term or fixed-task contract, end of a training contract, dismissal, redundancy, etc. The role of the personnel specialist in this context is to:

■ Conduct or advise on the conduct of termination interviews to ascertain the reasons behind any resignation and to tie up any loose ends.
■ In the event of redundancy, advise on possible alternatives and on the consultation and communication required.
■ Design a redundancy and severance policy and advise on its application and on termination payments.
■ Provide or advise on the provision of outplacement counselling.
■ Organize any necessary pre-retirement courses and provide advice as required.
■ In the event of any appeal on dismissal, advise managers of the actions to be taken.

TOPICAL ISSUES

HRM is a constantly changing and developing area. Some of the key issues currently being discussed by human resource specialists include the following:

■ The extent to which personnel activities should be undertaken by line managers.
■ How those line managers who are taking over personnel activities can be adequately trained to carry them out.
■ How the human resource function can be more closely integrated with the strategy and objectives of the organization.
■ The extent to which personnel activities should be outsourced or undertaken by contractors or consultants.
■ How the effectiveness of the personnel function can be assessed and demonstrated — a perennial problem this one, compounded by some recent studies, some demonstrating that organizations with a strong

personnel function are more effective and others showing that they are less effective!

- How to measure, develop and reward competencies, ie those observable and measurable behaviours required for effective or superior job performance.
- With organizations seeking to reduce costs and with leaner and less hierarchical structures, how it is possible to use people more flexibly and to get a higher level of performance from them while keeping them motivated, which has led to a focus on performance issues, multi-skilling and flexible systems of work.
- How to handle reductions in staffing levels and the problems of dealing with redundancy and outplacement.
- Growth in the complexity of managing people and the increased use of new technology have broadened the knowledge base required within the personnel function.
- Closer ties with the European Union have led to a more international approach and the growth of international 'Euro-managers', which itself brings a whole raft of new requirements in terms of service conditions and pay, etc.
- The degree to which the organization should have a single status and common conditions of employment for all staff.

Activity — HRM in your organization

1. Consider your own organization. What do you see as the key issues in human resource management? Compare your views with those of other managers.
2. To what extent do any of the activities listed in Table 1.1 below apply in your organization?

A recent study[3] of 560 employers carried out on behalf of the Leicestershire Training and Enterprise Council showed how frequently particular HRM initiatives were undertaken (see Table 1.1).

HUMAN RESOURCE MANAGEMENT IN EUROPE

There are a number of differences between the UK and the rest of Europe in the way that human resource management has developed in recent years[4]. Some examples of these recent developments are summarized below.

Germany

The HR environment in Germany is one of the most regulated in Europe[5]. This is largely because of the works councils, originally established in the 1950s and underpinned by legislation in 1972. Employers must get the

Table 1.1 *HRM activities*

Culture change programme — a planned attempt to alter attitudes, values and behaviour at work	35%
Devolved management — pushing responsibility down to lower levels	65%
Teamworking — among non-managerial employees	76%
Performance appraisal — for non-managerial employees	55%
Mission statement	42%
Team briefing	74%
Quality circles	35%
Harmonization of terms and conditions	40%
Psychometric tests	11%
Delayering — removal of one or more tiers of management	19%
Increased flexibility between jobs	75%

consent of their works council to appointments or dismissals, to set working hours, to introduce overtime or even to change the prices in the works canteen. Employees have legally guaranteed co-determination rights and also have the right to be consulted on business planning issues and to be given information on company performance.

Public companies have a two-tier structure which comprises a supervisory board, on which employees make up one-third or one-half of the membership and which in turn appoints the executive board. The supervisory board appoints the labour director who sits on the executive board and was originally there to represent the employees, but is now usually a personnel professional.

German unions are organized on an industry basis which means that there are far fewer of them than in the UK — there are only 17 affiliated to the DGB, the German equivalent of the Trades Union Congress (TUC). As a result Germany has had fewer demarcation disputes over the years.

This structure means that personnel professionals do not normally become involved in pay negotiation, but they do have to implement and interpret agreements in a very complex legislative environment. For this reason they often have a legal background. However, the Price Waterhouse–Cranfield Project[6] indicated that some 62 per cent of personnel managers in Germany were involved in developing corporate strategy compared to some 51 per cent in the UK.

In recruitment there is more emphasis on internal promotion and, compared with the UK, on training. To cope with skill shortages more use is now being made of flexible working.

France

In general, France has a far more regulated environment than the UK, with comprehensive legislation on work and social security and with other obligations imposed by long-standing agreements and custom and practice. One result of this is that as well as the normal HR functions there is usually someone with specific responsibility for industrial relations, the director of social affairs, whose prime responsibility is to oversee the wide range of committees of employee representatives and the operation of social security legislation within the organization. Collective agreements occupy a central place in French organizations and carry the weight of law.

The role of the director of social affairs in advising on these elements and managing the committees is seen as central, since infringement can mean fines or even prison for the company president or equivalent, which is where the ultimate responsibility lies. The committees comprise the works council, meetings of employee delegates which consider individual rather than company-wide problems, and health and safety committees. As in the UK, this highly regulated industrial relations environment has changed from one of confrontation to being more of a vehicle for communication and dialogue between the organization and its employees.

Many remuneration policies in French organizations are individualized and related to performance. However, at the top of the organization is what is known as a 'cadre', rather similar in status to managers in the UK but with a very specific set of agreements which confer special and more favourable benefits than those applying to other staff. For this reason there is no such thing as a single-status organization, ie one in which all employees are on the same terms and conditions. Similarly, as benefits are automatically allocated there is little opportunity to apply 'cafeteria' benefits, ie to offer employees a menu of benefits from which a selection can be made.

Spain

Much of Spain's HRM practice has been shaped by its political history and by the recent recovery in the economy[7]. The significant changes which have taken place over the years, coupled with the rapidly changing social environment, have meant that HRM in general, and executive development in particular, have become strategic priorities for organizations. There is, in particular, a realization that there is an increasing need for what are described as 'brainworkers', ie people who are technologically skilled, and to ensure that they are fully integrated into the organization.

Despite this there is evidence that only some 60 per cent of organizations have developed systematic training activities and that about one-third have no training plan.

Recruitment is carried out primarily through interviews, the main means of selection in some 80 per cent of companies, although a large number have started to use personality tests.

Spanish employers are making increasing use of variable pay with an estimated 60 per cent of companies operating some kind of financial incentive. Non-financial or fringe benefits are a popular way of supporting recruitment and retention strategies.

Employment law and industrial relations are governed by Spain's constitution, the civil code and workers' statutes. Industrial relations are still developing with a greater need for cooperation between management and unions.

Belgium

A great influence on HRM in Belgium is the cultural diversity of the country. With the Flemish in the north and the French-speaking Walloons in the south, as well as a number of mixed communities, there are inevitably a wide range of different organization cultures, personnel policies and procedures. This has tended to result in a pragmatic attitude to personnel management which is more likely to be judged on its contribution to organizational objectives.

Industrial relations operate very much on a basis of consultation and consensus with collective agreements made at industry, sector or national level having the force of law. These can be improved on at company level, with the role of the government seen as filling in the gaps not covered by agreements. The main drawbacks to this consensus approach are that it leads to compromise without any clear line of policy emerging and that activities have to be developed within a growing regulatory framework that is in danger of stifling initiative.

Another feature of the Belgian system is very high taxation, which at up to 55 per cent, plus social security contributions, is second only to Sweden in Europe. This makes it very difficult to introduce effective remuneration policies and human resource managers have to concentrate on finding tax-efficient benefits.

Generally personnel management is becoming increasingly integrated with the objectives of the organization and the responsibilities of line managers.

Italy

In Italy the personnel function has evolved from either the payroll or industrial relations activities, both of which are highly regulated[8]. Indeed there is generally a considerable amount of state intervention with three state-owned holding companies controlling large elements of industry in a number of diverse sectors. Similarly, there is a substantial amount of legislation covering employment rights, wages and prices. These extensive individual rights cover such things as index-linked pay, termination indemnities, and social security and pension provisions superior to those in the UK.

Minimum pay levels, cost of living increases and terms and conditions of employment are established through negotiations between employers' organizations and trade union confederations. All companies employing more than 15 people must have a works council which bargains at company level on collective agreements and represents individuals on grievance and disciplinary issues.

The emphasis in personnel management is on dealing with the works councils and interpreting legislation and national contracts. The highly regulated nature of pay and conditions means that there is relatively little scope for innovation in this area.

Despite this regulatory environment, or perhaps because of it, little is done according to the rule book. Many smaller companies, for example, prefer to subcontract or employ outworkers rather than pay social security contributions, but belong to cooperatives to achieve economies of scale. There is also a traditional mistrust of government and authority and Italians prefer to look after their own interests.

The Netherlands

While there are a number of similarities between the Netherlands and the UK in the way that human resource management has developed, there has perhaps been more emphasis in the Netherlands on industrial democracy and less on the extent to which human resource management can help to deliver corporate objectives. However, recent studies have shown that there is now a greater emphasis on the development of personnel and human resource management strategies, although there is still a reluctance to translate these into firm action plans and deadlines. Much of the current emphasis is on decentralization, quality control, quality certification, strategic human resource management and the implications of European integration.

A more competitive corporate environment means that there is a greater requirement for skilled and adaptable staff and more emphasis on training and development, human resource planning and procurement. There is also an increased dislike of bureaucracy and a greater readiness to contract out personnel tasks. In the chemical and plastics company DSM, for example, as part of a programme to be completed by 1995, out of an original personnel staff of 600, 245 are due to move to external contractors. Many of those remaining are to be deployed among business units or join an internal consultancy providing personnel services.

There is a tendency for organizations to work towards an integrated personnel function with relatively few specialists. This has led to a greater dependence on external specialists and the possible consequence that the value of the function is more difficult to demonstrate to line managers. As in the UK, the transfer of personnel functions to line managers has continued, with one study estimating that 58.7 per cent of organizations transferred personnel functions between 1985 and 1990.

Denmark

Workers in Denmark enjoy some of the most generous terms and conditions and are among the highest paid in Europe, so there is likely to be little difficulty for employers in complying with EC directives[9]. These conditions derive largely from the long tradition of collective agreements between employers and employees that have influenced employment law.

Danish line managers are more closely involved in day-to-day personnel management than managers in virtually any other country in Europe and for this reason their personnel departments tend to be smaller. For example, in the construction company Hoejgaard and Schultz, although there are over 3000 employees there are only five people in the central personnel department. Part of the reason for this advanced devolution of functions to line managers may be the similar backgrounds of personnel specialists and other managers. There is no equivalent in Denmark to the UK Institute of Personnel and Development (IPD) professional education scheme and many managers have general management qualifications which will have included a large element of personnel management.

Two other noticeable features are a strong commitment to employee development with up to 40 per cent of the workforce receiving training or retraining at any one time, and a lack of social distinctions, such as executive dining rooms.

Greece

Greece is very much the home of the small business. A study in 1988 showed that there were only 130 establishments with more than 500 staff but almost 500,000 with four staff or fewer[10]. These figures have apparently not changed significantly since then. Given this scenario it is not surprising that there are relatively few professional personnel functions. There is, furthermore, a strong patriarchal element with companies often being headed by the individual who built them, and being run in a very hands-on, autocratic way. Such leaders often concern themselves with every aspect of the business and delegate little or nothing.

Employment regulation includes elements of the constitution, laws and parts of laws, decrees and collective agreements. These have not been codified for many years so rules are vague and ill-defined. The emphasis in personnel management, therefore, has been on detailed administration and compliance.

THE STRUCTURE OF THE BOOK

All the chapters of this book are interrelated and there is no one particular order for reading them that can be described as the right one. However, generally the chapters have been set out in the order in which human resource activities would take place within a model organization. Life, of course, is nothing like as tidy, so there is no implication that these various activities are in any way as rigidly sequential in reality.

The chapters are as follows:

Chapter 2 — Human Resource Planning

This chapter describes the main processes used by organizations for planning their human resource requirements. Such planning should of course be a continuous process occurring at all stages of the organization's life as people come and go and business requirements change.

Chapter 3 — Job Analysis

Following a decision about its people requirements, the organization should begin the process for meeting them. Part of this process involves determining the appropriate structure and jobs. Chapter 3 therefore looks at the process of job analysis.

Chapter 4 — Recruitment and Selection

Having decided on the jobs to be filled and on the type of people required to fill them, the next step is to attract people to the organization and try to ensure that the best people are selected for the jobs available in the fairest way. The various stages of the process are covered in this chapter.

Chapter 5 — Performance Management

Crucial to the effectiveness of any organization is the performance of its staff. While this is an essential part of any line manager's role, a comprehensive performance management process has central implications for effective HRM and these are considered in this chapter.

Chapter 6 — Training and Development

Effective training and development is essential for staff to perform well and to ensure that the organization has people capable of meeting new challenges. This is considered in Chapter 6.

Chapter 7 — Job Evaluation

Part of the process of managing staff involves ensuring that there is equity of treatment, particularly in terms of pay and conditions. To achieve this pay equity, especially in large organizations, it is often necessary to have some kind of job evaluation methodology, and various approaches are considered in this chapter.

Chapter 8 — Pay and Benefits

The organization's reward strategy can assist greatly in attracting and retaining people of the right calibre and can also have a significant impact on profits. This chapter considers various approaches to pay.

Chapter 9 — Industrial Relations and Employee Communication

Effective relationships and communication with trade unions are important for harmonious relationships and can greatly help in forming a joint cooperative approach to managing the organization. This chapter examines these issues.

Chapter 10 — Employment Law

This chapter reviews the main features of current employment law in the UK and Europe.

Chapter 11 — Personnel Systems and Procedures

This chapter reviews those policies and procedures not covered in other chapters, with the emphasis very much on the administrative procedures underpinning HRM.

References

[1]   Hall, L (1993) 'The boss from Brazil', *Personnel Today*, October.

[2]   Torrington, D and Hall, L (1991) *Personnel Management — A New Approach*, 2nd edn, Prentice Hall, London.

[3]   Storey, J (1994) 'How new-style management is taking hold', *Personnel Management*, January.

[4]   Tyson, S, Lawrence, P, Poirson, P, Manzolini, L and Seferi, S V (1993) *Human Resources Management in Europe — Strategic Issues and Cases*, Kogan Page, London.

[5]   Arkin, A (1992) 'At work in the powerhouse of Europe', *Personnel Management*, February.

[6]   Price Waterhouse–Cranfield Project on International Human Resource Management, surveys 1991 and 1992, in 'New priorities for Dutch HRM', *Personnel Management*, December 1992.

[7]   Rodriguez, J (1991) 'Spanish customs', *Personnel Management*, April.

[8]   Caplan, J (1992) 'It's the climate that counts', *Personnel Management*, April.

[9]   Arkin, A (1992) 'The land of social welfare', *Personnel Management*, March.

[10] Ball, G (1992) 'The Spartan profession', *Personnel Management*, September.

Human Resource Planning

In an ideal world managers plan their human resource requirements, just as they plan any other resources. They try to ensure that they have the right numbers of people in the right place at the right time to deliver the organization's strategic plan. Then they turn to this plan, designed to deliver their goals and objectives, and, taking account of any financial and other constraints and of changes in the environment, analyse systematically their people requirements. They are also aware that this is a two-way process and that the availability of the required people will also affect the corporate plan. If there are likely to be certain skill shortages, consideration is given to strategies for tackling this problem, such as more flexible ways of working.

The reality tends often, perhaps usually, to be somewhat different, with human resource planning being rather more expedient and driven by short-term imperatives. However, along with finance, people are the most important resource the organization has, so it makes sense for them to be subject to the same degree of planning rigour as applies to money. This chapter examines the relationship of human resource planning to the other aspects of human resource management and reviews recommended approaches compared to what actually happens in practice.

THE MEANING AND PURPOSE OF HUMAN RESOURCE PLANNING

Definitions

The Institute of Personnel and Development describes human resource planning as:

> The systematic and continuing process of analysing an organization's human resource needs under changing conditions and developing personnel policies appropriate to the longer-term effectiveness of the organization. It is an integral part of corporate planning and budgeting procedures since human resource costs and forecasts both affect and are affected by longer-term corporate plans.

The key aspects of human resource planning from this definition are that:

- It is systematic and part of a conscious and planned process rather than something that happens almost by accident.
- It is a continuing process, because the organization and its objectives, and the environment in which it operates, are constantly changing.
- It is both short term and long term but with an emphasis on the need to plan for longer-term survival (and growth).
- It is closely related to, and should be integrated with, the corporate planning process, since this will determine the organization's policies and priorities which in turn will be affected by the availability of human resources.
- The resource requirements will need to be assessed in both qualitative and quantitative terms.
- The level of resources will depend on what can be afforded.
- The resources should be at the level required for organizational effectiveness.

It is also important to note that the planning process will be affected by the organization's core philosophy. While it may well be assumed that most organizations will seek to keep their staffing at the lowest possible level, primarily because of the cost of the resource, what is regarded as the optimum will depend on the level of service the organization is trying to provide. For example, if banks feel that Saturday opening is essential to maintain a competitive service, then they will need to provide staffing sufficient to cover this. Similarly, if stores wish to keep queues to a reasonable length they will need to provide the right numbers of staff at tills and checkouts. Determining the amount of time customers can reasonably be expected to wait and the staffing levels necessary to avoid excessive waiting time while minimizing costs entails making some fine judgements.

It is also the case that some organizations operate on the basis of staffing levels that are above the minimum strictly necessary for operational efficiency. In some local authorities, for example, where what are known as Direct Services Organizations have been established to provide services on the basis of compulsory competitive tendering, part of the operating conditions laid down by the council is often that there should be no compulsory redundancies. In practice, however, this is a difficult policy to apply as maintaining existing staffing levels is likely to make the DSO less competitive and the resulting loss of business could lead to redundancies anyway.

Another factor that will affect the organization's approach to human resource planning will be the extent to which it is labour or capital intensive. Where labour costs form a relatively low proportion of the total costs it is possible to be more relaxed about staffing levels. However, the reality is that organizations will nearly always seek to keep their labour costs to the minimum, whatever their proportion of total costs.

Human resource planning is both a necessary part of and a contributor to the strategic planning process, as it not only helps the organization determine the resources required to achieve objectives, but it also helps determine what can realistically be achieved with the resources available. In this sense human resource planning both affects and is affected by the organization's strategic plan. A case study setting out some of the issues that can typically arise, particularly where an organization is having to adapt to a changing market, is described below.

Case study — Planning human resource requirements to improve competitiveness

Legislation introduced over recent years has required more and more public sector bodies, particularly local authorities, to seek competitive tenders for a number of their services under what are known as compulsory competitive tendering (CCT) arrangements. This means that in-house services have to bid in competition with external contractors to continue providing those services. If they fail to gain the contract redundancies are likely to result.

One such organization had a number of vehicle workshops, servicing a large in-house fleet, that were likely to be subject to CCT. However, compared with external contractors hourly rates were high, productivity was low and there was a significant amount of vehicle down-time. Also the numbers, sizes and locations of the workshops were less than ideal. While some rationalization of workshop location was necessary, the real key to improving competitiveness lay in getting the right numbers of employees with the right skills and working at a more productive level. This involved taking account of the following factors:

- numbers of employees at each location;
- number of productive hours worked;
- ratio of direct to indirect (support) employees;
- pay rates;
- time spent servicing vehicles;
- standard measures from other studies (mainly Audit Commission parameters);
- potential competitors' rates.

With this information it was possible to put forward a number of options for improving the organization's competitiveness, most of which involved a combination of reduced employee numbers, a different skills mix and reduced times for different servicing jobs.

Purposes of human resource planning

The main reasons for undertaking human resource planning are to ensure that the organization:

- is able to attract and retain staff in sufficient numbers and with the appropriate skills to be able to operate effectively and achieve its corporate objectives;
- fully utilizes the staff employed;
- is able to ensure that employees receive all the training and development necessary for effective performance in their current roles and develop the flexibility to be able to undertake other roles as the need arises;

- is able to anticipate and meet changes in the demand for its services or in the labour supply;
- is able to meet future human resource requirements from its own internal resources;
- ensures that equal opportunities for promotion and development are available to staff, particularly women, members of ethnic minorities and the disabled.
- keeps control of human resource costs and effectively anticipates the staffing costs of any new initiatives.

PROBLEMS OF HUMAN RESOURCE PLANNING

Human resource planning is more complex than planning other resources, such as finance, because:

- People are unpredictable — they can easily upset plans through resigning, being sick, refusing to do certain things, etc.
- People are all different so it is difficult to produce policies and approaches that are equally appropriate to all.
- The organization's requirement is not for a certain quantity of a homogeneous product but for different numbers of very specific types of people such as accountants, secretaries, electricians, etc.
- People are required in a particular place at a particular time and are less easy to move from one location to another than, say, money.
- Surpluses and deficits are more difficult to manage — staff numbers cannot usually be reduced at the stroke of a pen and acquiring more people can be time consuming and costly.
- People need careful and sensitive handling which requires substantial thought and care on the part of managers.
- There are more environmental conditions to take into account — money can be kept in a safe but people need offices, car parks, canteens, etc.

It is probably the combination of the above complexities that makes detailed and comprehensive human resource planning such a comparative rarity in organizations.

PLANNING PROCESSES

Any human resource planning process has to take account of the organization's likely future demand for labour and of the potential supply of labour. It can therefore be considered under the main headings of:

- *Demand forecasting* — which entails estimating the organization's future staffing requirements in terms of numbers and skills, by reference to its aims and objectives, and taking account of changes in working practices and activity levels.

■ *Supply forecasting* — which entails estimating the likely future labour supply, both from within the organization taking account of employee wastage, current skills mix, performance, etc, and from outside the organization taking account of the potential pool of staff with the right levels of knowledge and skill.

A simplified diagram illustrating the HR planning process is shown in Figure 2.1.

DEMAND FORECASTING

Methods of forecasting the demand for human resources can be broadly divided into the softer, subjective approaches and the harder, more objective ones. Both these kinds of approach are inherent in the techniques outlined below.

Managerial judgement

This is perhaps the most common subjective approach to forecasting demand, certainly in smaller organizations. It involves managers deciding, possibly in consultation with other staff in the organization, what their future activities are likely to be and how many and what types of staff they will need to be able to undertake these activities. This approach can be top-down, in which senior managers prepare forecasts based on the organization's corporate plan; or bottom-up, in which line and operating managers submit plans for approval by the top management; or a combination of the two.

With an increasing emphasis on the need to build empowered teams and

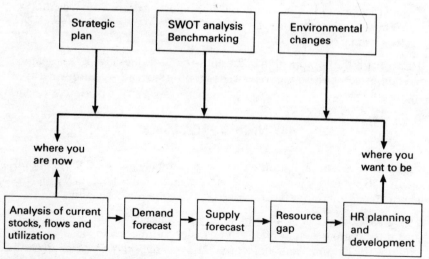

Figure 2.1 *Human resource planning process*

to reflect more closely the demands of customers (the inverted pyramid concept), there is perhaps a greater tendency to move towards a more bottom-up approach. In reality a combination of the two is the more logical option. Top managers should give guidance and direction on the projected resourcing levels expected for budgeted demand, but this should be based on consideration of feedback received from the 'coal-face'.

The degree to which this process is structured or formalized will vary from organization to organization and will depend on the other types of management process in place. Where there is some kind of priority-based budgeting system, for example, this will help the planning process but also make it more formal and structured.

The greatest problem with the use of managerial judgement is that it does rely on that judgement and may not be effective at dealing with situations that are outside the managers' experience. On the other hand, managers are paid to make just these kinds of decision and even with the most rigorous and objective approach a managerial decision still has to be made at some stage. Certainly, the approach does have the advantages that it is relatively straightforward and can be implemented quickly.

Ratio trend analysis

Ratio trend analysis involves reviewing the ratios between different groups of workers and projecting how these might change for different levels of output — for example, the number of supervisory staff required for different numbers of operatives. The projections will take account of any likely changes in technology or working methods. While this approach might be useful for dealing with the implications of some changes in production levels, it is really only appropriate where there is a direct relationship between job categories and where fairly large numbers are involved. It is, of course, also based on the assumption that the present staffing levels are correct.

Ratios can be a very useful means of estimating approximate staff numbers where there are activities for which standard productivity measures are available. For example, there are standard measures for the number of keystrokes that can be achieved by word processor operators within a given time, or the number of invoices that can be checked in a particular period. Similarly, when IBM was considering reducing its workforce it took the view that the ratio of support employees to front-line staff in the non-manufacturing part of the business had to be reduced from 55 per cent in 1989 to 35 per cent by mid-1992[1].

While such techniques are quick and easy to apply, they do rely on having accurate records and on accurate predictions of future workloads.

Work study

Work study techniques can be used to measure how long in terms of standard hours it will take to complete certain tasks. From this the employer can calculate how many employees will be needed to achieve the required levels of productivity, taking account of potential levels of absenteeism and other factors, such as availability of stores and machine downtime. While work study is usually directed at manual and craft work it can also be used to measure clerical work.

The main disadvantage of work study as a planning tool is that it can only really be used to measure standard tasks. Problems arise when attempts are made to measure more nebulous aspects of work such as the time taken to find faults in equipment, or where the jobs are less prescribed in nature, such as administrative or professional posts.

Modelling

A model is a simulation of a real-life situation built to include a number of interacting variables which can then be manipulated to answer 'what if . . .' type questions. If the organization has detailed personnel information this can be fed into the model and various projections made. This is relatively easy if computerized systems are used.

The types of raw data typically fed into such a model might include:

- numbers and types of staff in various job categories;
- grades, pay ranges or pay rates of the various jobs;
- numbers of new recruits, leavers and absence levels for each job category;
- ages and length of service of employees;
- assumptions about future developments within the organization.

There are a number of such models commercially available.

SUPPLY FORECASTING

An analysis of the supply of employees to the organization will need to take account of a number of factors:

- Existing staff levels categorized by function, department, job type, and pay or grade.
- An analysis of job requirements in terms of knowledge, qualifications, skills and experience.
- An analysis of the attributes of individual postholders in terms of age, length of service, qualifications, training, experience, skills and performance rating.
- Recruitment and retention rates, wastage rates and absence levels.
- Promotion rates.
- Any potential changes to working methods or demand for services and products.
- Available sources of supply from both within and outside the organization.

Statistical analysis can be undertaken for any of the above factors to predict potential changes. Much of the information mentioned will be required for other purposes, such as planning training programmes, succession planning or performance management, so should be readily available within the organization.

There are a number of conventional ways of measuring these factors and they are set out below.

Staff turnover or wastage

It is important for any organization to measure its employee turnover as this will enable it to plan its recruitment programme. It can also be an important measure of the organization's health as a high turnover can indicate that something is amiss. Too high a turnover will entail substantial additional recruitment and training costs, as well as possible loss of productivity and damage to staff morale.

For this reason, it is not just the rate of turnover that should be measured but also the reasons for it, ideally by conducting exit interviews with staff who leave. Such interviews are often effective at drawing attention to problems that might not have otherwise come to light, and can sometimes have the effect of making the person concerned change his or her mind about leaving.

Turnover Index

The usual formula for measuring turnover is as follows:

$$\frac{No.\ of\ leavers\ in\ year}{Average\ no.\ of\ staff\ in\ post\ during\ year} \times 100 = \%\ wastage$$

While this is a very useful and widely used measure it needs to be treated with a degree of caution, since a very high turnover in a small part of the organization — perhaps for a very legitimate reason — could distort the figure for the organization as a whole. Also repeated filling of just a few jobs could similarly distort the overall picture.

Stability Index

The stability index measures the degree of continuity in the organization by measuring the number of staff tending to remain in it. The formula is:

$$\frac{No.\ of\ staff\ with\ at\ least\ one\ year's\ service}{No.\ of\ staff\ employed\ one\ year\ ago} \times 100 = \%\ stability$$

The main disadvantage of this approach is that it takes only limited account of service and does not highlight the very different situations that can exist between organizations with a high number of long-serving employees and those with more short-service employees.

Length of service analysis

To overcome the disadvantages of the stability index an analysis can be made of the average length of service of people who leave the organization. Bowey[2] recommends the following formula:

$$\frac{\textit{Length of service in months over two years of all current staff added together}}{\textit{Length of service in months over two years of a full complement of staff added together}} \times 100 = \% \textit{ stability}$$

Cohort or survival analysis

Cohort or survival analysis entails keeping track of a homogeneous group within the organization to determine how many of that group remain after a certain period. This might, for example, be applied to a group of trainees who join the organization at the same time. The main features of this approach are that it is applied to groups who have common characteristics and it must cover the same period of time. The results can be plotted on a graph or as a curve as illustrated in Figure 2.2.

Plotting these curves can give an indication to the organization of how many of a certain group of staff might have to be recruited to meet its human resource requirements in the future.

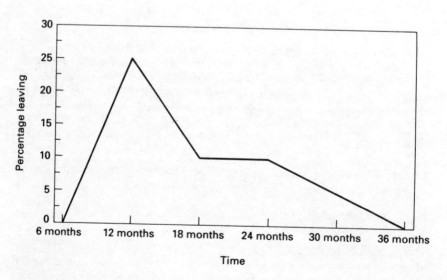

Figure 2.2 *A survival curve*

Half-life index

This index defines the time taken for half a cohort to leave the organization through wastage. This gives less information than the cohort analysis but is useful for comparing different groups and years.

Census method

This method analyses leavers over a relatively short period, such as a year, and records the length of completed service. This can then be plotted on a frequency histogram or graph. This should help to show any patterns that may need to be investigated by the organisation, eg an exceptionally high loss of people with long service.

Retention Profile

Staff remaining in the organization are placed in groups depending on their year of joining and then the number in each group is expressed as a percentage of the total number of joiners during that year. This shows the tendency for employees to remain with the organization and can assist in succession planning.

Other techniques

A number of other human resource planning techniques have been used by different organizations at different times. Some of these derive from mathematical or accountancy models and others are linked to salary planning or analysis of promotions and other personnel data.

Changes in working methods and practices

In planning human resource requirements managers should not only take account of all the factors likely to affect recruitment and retention rates, but should also give fundamental consideration to working methods and practices. Certainly before rushing to fill vacancies or create redundancies, consideration should be given to alternative ways of achieving the same outputs. Similarly, high staff turnover and low retention rates can be

---

Activity — Staff turnover and stability

Consider your organization:

1. What is the annual staff turnover?
2. What are the reasons for staff leaving?
3. Are these reasons recorded and analysed?
4. Are there any clear patterns, such as a particularly high rate of turnover in one department?
5. What steps can be taken to reduce turnover?

indicative of many different problems, among which might be included dissatisfaction with the methods of working.

The main approaches to consider are as follows:

- More flexible patterns of work and greater interchangeability between jobs.
- Introducing new systems of work, including new technology.
- Reorganizing work.
- Changing the organization's structure.
- Using alternatives to full-time employees, such as temporary staff, contractors, job-sharing or part-time staff.
- Encouraging more homeworking and teleworking.
- Introducing productivity schemes.
- Retraining and developing staff.
- Changing the organization's culture.
- Changing working hours through overtime, shift working, flexible hours schemes, annual hours, etc.
- More management training and development.

The key point is that in planning the organization's human resource requirements, consideration has to be given not just to the existing and projected numbers of staff, but also to productivity and performance, as these will have a profound effect on the numbers and types of jobs required. Getting the numbers right is part of the battle, but it is equally important to ensure that staff are highly motivated and trained and that working methods are those which are most appropriate.

Sources of supply

The sources of labour supply to the organization are both internal and external. The organization should have good information available about the internal supply, from such sources as personnel records which should contain details of previous experience and qualifications, training records and performance appraisal forms, which might also give promotability ratings. From these sources managers will be able to gain a good idea of the likelihood of meeting future requirements from the internal supply.

Analysing the external labour market is more difficult and it may not always be possible to recruit easily people with the right attributes, the only option often being for the organization to 'grow its own'. In considering the potential supply of labour the following factors should be taken into account:

- The location of the organization and the general perception of the area.
- Accessibility by public transport.
- The likely skills available in the local population and traditional working patterns.
- The local unemployment level.
- Proximity to large population centres.

- Competition from other employers.
- The competitiveness of the organization's pay and benefits levels.
- Local educational facilities.
- Government policies, statutes, training initiatives, etc.
- The organization's image.
- Demographic changes.
- Changes in the industrial and commercial make-up of the area.

RETAINING STAFF

Whether it is regarded as part of the planning process, or more a question of effective performance management, it is important for the organization to incorporate a retention strategy. Failure to do so could result in high turnover rates. Common issues affecting employee turnover include:

- *Pay and benefits* — these should be perceived internally as fair, as considerable dissatisfaction can arise if people do not feel that they are being treated as well as their colleagues. Similarly, if the organization does not pay as well as its competitors it may well lose staff over time.
- *Recognition and prospects* — wherever possible the management's appreciation should be conveyed for a job well done. Effective workers should be promoted where possible, provided they are equipped to do the next job, but in the absence of such opportunities praise is always welcome.
- *Working conditions* — poor working conditions will cause dissatisfaction.
- *Job design* — the jobs themselves should be designed to suit the individual as far as possible and should provide variety, interest and opportunities for learning and growth, otherwise dissatisfaction is likely to result.
- *Working relationships* — poor working relationships will cause upsets and result in absenteeism and increased staff turnover.
- *Performance* — if people feel inadequate or not up to the job morale will suffer, so they must be given clear guidance on what is expected of them and any necessary training.
- *Commitment* — if people do not feel committed to the organization they will pursue their own agendas. It is for the managers to explain the organization's purpose and objectives and to try to gain commitment to them.
- *Poor selection and promotion* — appointing someone who is not ready for the job he or she is asked to do may well result in rapid turnover, of this member of staff or others.
- *Expectations* — if expectations are raised about progress within the organization or about the rewards available, but then are not met, the resulting disillusion can lead to increased turnover.
- *Ineffective supervision or management.*

The planning process, therefore, will need to incorporate plans for:

- the supply of human resources;
- organization and structure;
- recruitment and retention;
- employee utilization and flexibility;
- training and development;
- communication;
- performance management;
- rewards.

COSTING HUMAN RESOURCE REQUIREMENTS

One of the main reasons it is necessary to plan human resources effectively is that they are a very significant part of almost any organization's costs. Some of the costs that need to be taken into account as part of the process are as follows:

- Basic pay and bonuses, profit related pay, overtime, shift payments, cash supplements, etc.
- Benefits such as cars, health insurance, holidays, pension and share options.
- Statutory costs such as national insurance, pension contributions and maternity pay.
- Recruitment advertising.
- Preparing job descriptions and personnel specifications.
- Staff time spent interviewing, etc.
- Possible cost of employing selection consultants.
- Medical examinations.
- Training costs including salaries, training materials and equipment, accommodation costs, lower productivity during training and costs of trainers.
- Relocation costs including expenses associated with moving and loans.
- Leaving costs such as redundancy, severance, outplacement, loss of productivity during notice period.
- Fringe benefits, eg sports and social facilities, staff restaurant and awards for long service.
- Personnel administration costs.

Any human resource planning process will need to take into account all the above costs and any others associated with the employment process, because of their potential as key measures in analysing business performance and developing future strategy.

References

[1]   Peach, Sir Leonard (1992) 'Parting by mutual agreement: IBM's transition to manpower cuts', *Personnel Management*, March.

[2]   Bowey, A (1974) *A Guide to Manpower Planning*, Macmillan, London.

Job Analysis

This chapter is concerned with the process of analysing jobs in the organization. Jobs are the basic components of the organization's structure and are the means by which it achieves its objectives. It follows, therefore, that for any organization to be successful it must give a great deal of care and attention to the way in which jobs are designed. A good person–job fit, which is generally recognized as essential for motivated and high-performing staff, can only be achieved if there is sufficient clarity about the job in question. The various stages in the process of job analysis are summarized in Figure 3.1.

Although the emphasis in this chapter is on the more traditional and more widely used approaches to job analysis which focus on the content of

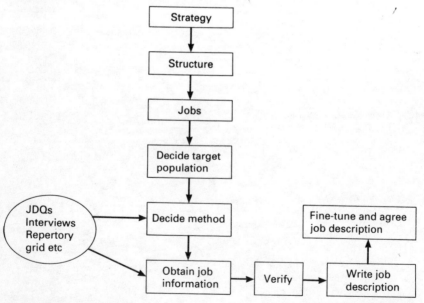

Figure 3.1 *The job analysis process*

jobs, the competency approach, which focuses on the people rather than the jobs, is also discussed.

DEFINITIONS

Job analysis

Job analysis is a process used to determine and describe the content of jobs in such a way that a clear understanding of what the job is about is communicated to anyone who might require the information for management purposes.

Job description

A job description is a written statement of the content of any particular job derived from the analysis of that job.

Personnel specification

Whereas the job description describes the content of a particular job, the personnel or person specification describes the attributes required of an employee to carry out the job described to a satisfactory standard.

Competency

A competency is defined by Boyatzis[1] as an underlying characteristic of an individual which is causally related to effective or superior performance in a job. Differentiating competencies distinguish superior from average performers and those required for adequate or average performance are described as threshold or essential competencies.

USES OF JOB ANALYSIS

There are a number of reasons for analysing jobs. The main uses to the organization are as follows:

- Human resource planning.
- Selection.
- Job evaluation.
- Training and development.
- Job redesign.
- Performance management.
- Organization review and restructuring.
- Employees' rights.

These are considered in turn below.

Human resource planning

Once an organization has agreed its strategy and objectives, the next stage is to plan the resources required to meet those objectives. In terms of employees, this means ensuring that there are the appropriate numbers of people with the right skills, knowledge and experience in the right place, at the right time. This entails, first, deciding what needs to be achieved in terms of outputs, and then making a decision about the numbers and types of job required to achieve these outputs. This might mean designing an entirely new job or jobs, or changing existing jobs to meet new demands. Either way it is imperative for these purposes that the organization has good analytical data about its jobs.

Selection

Before any post can be filled it is important for the organization to have a clear idea of the requirements of that job. Without this information it would be difficult to know what qualifications, experience and personal attributes to look for, or what to pay. By producing a job description and a personnel specification the organization will be better able to decide how and by whom any particular job should be filled.

Job evaluation

One of the main reasons for undertaking any job analysis exercise is so that jobs can be properly evaluated. Without good information, however, it is very unlikely that any job evaluation exercise will give fair and accurate results. While it may be possible to be somewhat less precise about the requirements when planning human resource needs or when filling jobs, any vagueness will undermine the efficacy of a job evaluation process.

Training and development

It is important to identify the content of jobs when analysing training needs, as without this information it will be difficult to specify the outputs, standards of performance and competencies required. When accurate job information is available any mismatch between the expected outputs and individual performance is easier to identify.

Job redesign

Organizations are changing ever more rapidly, particularly with current tendencies towards delayering and greater flexibility in jobs. Consideration has frequently to be given to the reallocation of duties and responsibilities and to the possibility of different ways of working. To make these decisions effectively, good information is required about the activities currently undertaken within jobs.

Performance management

Performance management (see Chapter 5) is a process for ensuring that the performance of individual postholders is effectively managed and that they perform to their maximum effectiveness. To measure and appraise performance it is necessary to compare the requirements of the job with the extent to which the individual meets those requirements. This necessitates that job objectives are clearly specified, as without clarity in this area no performance management process will be fully effective.

Organization review and restructuring

When organization structures and reporting lines are being changed, it is important to have good information about the content of all jobs. In this way, duplications and overlaps of responsibility can be identified and managers can ensure that no vital processes or tasks are omitted.

Employees' rights

While there is no legal requirement to give an employee a job description (although there is a requirement to describe the job briefly or to indicate the job title), it is sound management to do so to reduce ambiguity, on either side, about what the postholder is required to do. Vagueness in this area could cause problems in any subsequent issues relating to grievances, discipline, redundancy or termination of employment. The content of the job description forms part of the terms and conditions of employment and is part of the contractual relationship between the employee and the employer.

Notwithstanding these comments, it should be recognized that individuals alter the jobs they are doing so it is difficult to have complete clarity about the content of any job.

INFORMATION TO BE OBTAINED

Job analysis will typically be used to obtain the following information:

- *Job identification* — this includes the title of the job, the department or section, any employee or job number and the name of the postholder (which is often kept confidential in a job evaluation exercise to reduce subjectivity).
- *Reporting relationships* — that is, the title of the post to which the job directly reports, the jobs reporting directly to this one, any major coordination links and any functional, as opposed to line, relationships.
- *Job content* — including the main purpose of the job, the boundaries of the job in terms of authority, and the specific accountabilities or tasks to be undertaken.

- *Performance measures and standards* — the outputs expected from the job and the standard to which they should be performed, sometimes described as key result areas.
- *Personal characteristics* — the knowledge, skills and experience required of the postholder to meet the requirements of the job fully.
- *Constraints* — in terms of the limits of authority and the decision-making freedom of the post.
- *Relevant statistics* — details of any budgets, equipment and other resources for which the post might be responsible or data relating to outputs and workload.
- *Working conditions* — any information about the working environment or any special conditions attaching to the job.
- *Other information* — this can include anything else that may be relevant to the job such as any training requirements, additional responsibilities that may not be a permanent feature, or any other special factors.

PRINCIPLES OF JOB ANALYSIS

The key principles underlying job analysis are as follows:

1. *Analysis not list of tasks.* The analysis of the job should break it down into its component parts and not just list the activities carried out. This entails fully describing the various aspects of the job in a way that gives a clear picture of what the jobholder actually does and how the activities fit together, that describes the complexities and challenges of the job, and that makes it clear what the job contributes to the organization. Mere lists do not help in giving an understanding of what the job is about.
2. *Jobs not people.* The analysis is of the job, not how an individual performs in that job. The analysis should take account of the knowledge, skills and experience required but should not record what the jobholder actually has, which may be different from what is required. However, it is as well to be aware that job content is affected by many different factors, as Figure 3.2 indicates.
3. *Non-judgemental.* In analysing the job, the analyst is only concerned with the actual content and not the appropriateness and logic of that content (unless the analysis is part of an organization review). While apparent anomalies are worth noting they are an issue for the organization, not the person analysing the job.
4. *The job as it is today.* The analysis should only take account of the job content as it currently is, disregarding any possible future changes which may not actually happen, and excluding anything which might have happened in the past but which is no longer part of the job.

TECHNIQUES OF JOB ANALYSIS

There are a number of techniques of job analysis which may either be used

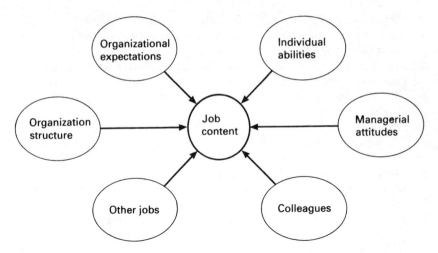

Figure 3.2 *Some influences on job content*

on their own or as just one of a number of different approaches. In many situations it may be necessary to use a combination of techniques to obtain the required information.

Interviews

The interview is one of the main ways of obtaining information about a job. Generally, the analyst will interview the postholder and this should result in the preparation of a job description. This will then be confirmed with the interviewee's immediate supervisor and any necessary changes made. The final document should be one that is agreed by all parties.

To obtain information successfully by this means the following guidelines should be adopted:

1. Prepare for the interview by researching the relevant aspects of the organization, function and job under consideration.
2. Prepare a list of questions and, as far as possible, follow a logical structure during the interview.
3. Ensure that the interview is properly organized and held somewhere that is free from interruption.
4. Interviewees will often be apprehensive and defensive and so time must be taken to try to relax them as much as possible.
5. Explain the purpose of the interview and stress that you are seeking facts not opinions.
6. Try to ensure that the answers you are given are facts and not judgements.
7. Remember that most (though by no means all) postholders are likely to exaggerate their role, so ensure that any vague or general answers are clarified.

8. Ask open-ended questions that invite people to describe what they do, rather than closed questions that invite a reply of 'yes' or 'no'.
9. Avoid asking leading questions that imply what the answer should be.
10. Encourage an atmosphere in which the postholder is happy to talk.
11. Wherever possible get examples of the kinds of things the postholder actually does, as this will help to give a better idea of the overall job.
12. Obtain clear information about the postholder's limits of authority, decisions made, when matters have to be referred to superiors, etc.
13. Take comprehensive notes of what is said during the interview.
14. Summarize regularly to test your understanding of what has been said.
15. At the end of the interview ask the interviewee whether there are any other points that need to be added.
16. Explain to the interviewee the next stage in the process and reserve the right to talk to him or her again should you require any further information or need to clarify any points.
17. Thank the person concerned for his or her cooperation.
18. Review and write up your notes as soon as possible after the interview.
19. Prepare the job description and check the content with the interviewee.

The main drawbacks to interviews are that they can be time consuming, and therefore costly, and the accuracy of their results depends on the skill of the interviewer and the honesty and clarity of the interviewee.

Self-reports

Jobholders can be asked to describe their jobs and to prepare job descriptions. However, there will inevitably be a substantial variation in the way in which these are written, especially if no clear guidelines are given, and the quality of the information will depend significantly on the writing skills of the jobholder. Such an approach will therefore require the jobholders to be given clear training and guidance.

Questionnaires

Questionnaires are one of the most widely used ways of obtaining information about jobs, especially where there is a large job population to cover. It is a less time-consuming and costly way of obtaining information than by interviewing. By using a structured approach it is possible to gain a greater consistency in the standard of answers and ensure that all the required information is obtained. There are a number of proprietary tools available, among the best known of which are the Position Analysis Questionnaire (PAQ)[2] and Saville and Holdsworth's Work Profiling System. The PAQ analyses jobs in terms of:

■ information input — where and how the worker gets information used in the job;

- mental processes — what reasoning, decision making, planning, etc are involved in the job;
- work output — what physical activities are performed and what tools or equipment are used;
- relationships with others required in the job;
- job context in both physical and social terms;
- other job characteristics.

The greatest constraint on the use of questionnaires is the extent to which people are willing and able to complete them. When completed they should be signed by the jobholder and the line manager and dated.

Checklists

A checklist comprises a list of items that might apply to a particular job, and the jobholder and his or her supervisor is required to tick only those items that apply to the job in question. Checklists are particularly useful where there are a large number of routine jobs all carrying out similar tasks and where these tasks are of a straightforward nature.

Checklists are easy and quick to complete and can therefore be a rapid way of obtaining information about a large number of jobs. The main problem is that they need to be carefully prepared to ensure that the right information is obtained and that nothing vital is missed, otherwise they will not give a true and complete picture of any particular job.

Diaries and logs

Work diaries and logs can be used to compile a record of a postholder's daily activities. The approach is more valuable for higher-level and managerial jobs but is a very time-consuming process, relying on the dedication and accuracy of the postholder completing the record, and the results can be difficult to analyse.

Observation

Observation is generally regarded as one of the most accurate ways of obtaining job information and has underpinned many of the work study schemes introduced over the years. However, it is a time-consuming and costly process. There is also the danger that those observed might change their behaviour because of the process itself, sometimes described as the Hawthorne effect (a term derived from a series of experiments conducted at the Western Electric Company in the United States in the 1920s and 1930s).

Participant observation

Participant observation involves the analyst actually carrying out the job to obtain information about it. Again this can be time consuming and there is the danger that if insufficient time is allotted the analyst might fail to appreciate certain aspects of the job. There is the further question of whether such an approach would be seen as credible in the eyes of others working in the same environment.

Critical incident method

The critical incident method is one in which jobholders are asked to recall critical incidents that have occurred in the performance of the job undertaken. In this way it is hoped to build up a picture of the key aspects of the job that are related to success or failure. It is particularly valuable when analysing behaviours for the purpose of preparing competency definitions, and a variant of this is the behavioural event interview (see below). The main drawbacks to this kind of approach are that it is highly dependent on the accuracy of recall of the interviewee, and it tends to disregard some of the more mundane, but nevertheless important aspects of the job.

Hierarchical task analysis

Under this approach jobs are broken down into a hierarchical set of tasks, which are then in turn broken down into subtasks. These are defined in terms of their objectives or outputs and also the way in which these are to be achieved. The process entails describing what needs to be done, the standards to which it has to be done, and any conditions associated with task performance.

Repertory grid

The repertory grid technique focuses on job content by differentiating between good and poor performers. It is a way of obtaining personal constructs, which are individuals' views about the world. For example, an analyst might interview a manager to obtain views about a particular job. By asking the manager to make a series of judgements about the individuals carrying out this job, based on what differentiates their respective performances, and isolating these actions, it is possible to build up a picture of what is required for effective job performance.

Such an approach is time consuming and requires considerable analytical skill on the part of the interviewer, but it can provide a great deal of valuable information.

Competence assessment

The assessment of competence would typically involve the following steps[3]:

1. Defining performance effectiveness criteria, eg sales, profits, productivity, ratings by peers, customers, subordinates, etc.
2. Defining a criterion sample of superior performers, such as the top 10 per cent of those achieving specified targets.

3. Data collection through a variety of means. These can include:
   - Expert panels or focus groups who describe the competencies they think are required for average and for superior performance (most people can readily agree about the high performers in any organization).
   - Surveys and 360 degree ratings (involving jobholders, superiors, peers, clients) in which observers who know the job are asked to identify the specific behaviours defining competencies.
   - An expert system database containing data from numerous competency models and providing computer-generated competency definitions.
   - Behavioural event interviews (BEIs) which give detailed narrative accounts of how both superior and average performers thought and acted during critical incidents in their jobs, including successes and failures.
   - Observation in which both superior and average performers are studied in actual or simulated work situations.
4. Data analysis and identification of the competencies required for average and superior performance, typically presented as a scale.
5. Validation of the predictive validity of the competency model using a second sample of jobholders and supported by psychometric tests, assessment centres and BEIs.

Some of the core competencies identified for managers in a large organization are set out in the example below.

Core competencies for Argos Plc[4]
- Will to win
- Corporateness
- Initiating change
- Implementing change
- Teamwork
- Communication
- Leadership
- Commercial acumen
- Functional competence
- Resilience

WRITING JOB DESCRIPTIONS

Once a job has been analysed it is usual to produce a job description. The actual format of the job description and the content of it will depend on the job being described and the uses to which the job description is to be put. It should be borne in mind that job descriptions can be used for recruitment, job evaluation, training and development, performance appraisal, organization review, etc. They can also form part of the terms and conditions under which an individual is employed and are strong evidence of the organization's requirements in terms of the job outputs expected from a particular person.

Preparing good job descriptions is not an entirely straightforward task and they can suffer from a number of weaknesses. These are as follows:

- The quality of the content of the job description will depend strongly on the method of job analysis used and on the skills of the analyst, with any weaknesses in the analytical process being transmitted automatically to the description.

- If job descriptions are written over-rigidly, they could inhibit the organization's flexibility.

- In modern delayered organizations with empowered work teams, employees may be used very flexibly and more according to their abilities than in terms of the specific job they were engaged to do; this can be difficult to reflect in a description of specific job accountabilities or tasks.

- Job descriptions can rapidly become out of date and therefore need to be reviewed regularly.

The very process of preparing job descriptions can bring to light organizational anomalies and differences of viewpoint about such issues as reporting lines and job content.

Generally, when writing job descriptions it is important to be aware of the reason for preparing them and it clearly makes sense for them to be written in such a way as to have as many uses as possible.

The content of job descriptions

The precise content of any job description will vary according to the job, the organization and the environment. There is generally a tendency for jobs to be described in terms of inputs, ie what the postholder actually does, rather than in terms of outputs, ie why he or she does it. In practice, some jobs involve the individual in carrying out a number of routine tasks and all that is necessary in these circumstances is for those tasks to be clearly described. Other, less routine jobs are more likely to be driven by the need to attain certain objectives or outputs, and these should be described in terms of accountabilities, ie not only what the postholder does but why he or she does it. An extract from an accountabilities-based job description for a personnel director is shown in the example for Up and Down Lifts.

Most job descriptions, depending on the precise reason for preparing them, should generally contain the following:

Job title

The precise title of the job should be described briefly but accurately. A vague description such as 'manager' will be inadequate, unless there is only one post with that particular title.

Up and Down Lifts — Job Description Extract

Job:	Personnel Director
Jobholder:	Lesley Smith
Reports to:	Chief Executive
Date:	June 1994

Purpose
To help ensure that the company achieves its corporate objectives and makes the best use of its employees by developing and maintaining innovative, effective and forward-looking human resource strategies, practices and procedures.

Dimensions
1. Employees — 215 full-time equivalents (as at June 1994).
2. Payroll — £5.2 million.
3. Departmental budget — £230,000 p.a.

Principal Accountabilities
1. Develop and maintain appropriate and effective personnel strategies and ensure that these are communicated and implemented throughout the company in a way that supports corporate objectives.
2. Develop and maintain all necessary personnel planning, recruitment and selection procedures to ensure that the company has staff of the right calibre to enable it to meet its corporate objectives.
3. Develop and maintain a remuneration strategy and appropriate terms and conditions of employment to ensure that the company is able to attract, retain and motivate staff.
4. Advise the senior managers of the company about the personnel policies, procedures and actions required to ensure that the company makes the best use of its employees.
5. Develop and maintain all necessary training policies and procedures to ensure that all staff are trained and developed to the standards required.
6. Maintain an awareness of the requirements of employment legislation to ensure that the company complies with all legal requirements and to provide sound advice to management.
7. Encourage and maintain sound employee relations by undertaking all necessary consultation and negotiation with employee representatives and by ensuring the effective communication of company policies.
8. Develop and maintain all necessary personnel procedures and information systems to ensure that the company has all the information required for effective resource planning and management.
9. Direct and control the staff of the personnel group to ensure that they undertake their responsibilities effectively and within budget.

Job identification details

This will include any employee or job number that helps to identify the post in question.

Name of postholder

The name of the person occupying a particular job would normally be inserted, particularly if the job description is to be used for training or appraisal purposes, but is very likely to be omitted in any job evaluation (or recruitment) exercise.

Reporting line

The post to which the postholder normally reports will usually be included, or a relevant organization chart could be attached to, or included as part of, the job description.

Main purpose of job

It is usually helpful to summarize in one or two sentences the main reason for the job's existence. This should capture the job's unique contribution to the organization and answer by implication the question of what would happen, or not happen, if the job did not exist.

Tasks or accountabilities

The main part of the job description will usually set out the tasks or the main accountabilities undertaken by the postholder. Lists of tasks will normally be more appropriate for routine task-based jobs and where the main purpose of the job description is to give the jobholder clear guidelines on the work to be undertaken. More senior managerial and professional people will usually be employed to achieve objectives, rather than to carry out specific tasks, and it is more appropriate to write the job descriptions for them in terms of accountabilities or responsibilities. Where they are written in terms of accountabilities there should be no more than ten, as any greater number is likely to mean that the description is going into too much detail.

Context

There needs to be some description of the context in which the job is carried out. While this may be covered under a number of different headings, the main objective is to describe how work is processed, where it comes from and goes to, any special environmental considerations affecting the job, how the job fits into the rest of the section and the organization, etc.

Contacts

The main lines of communication of the job with other jobs in the organization and with external individuals and organizations, and the reasons for those links should be listed. It is wise to avoid the use of the overworked word 'liaison', as this can mean anything from high-powered and critical negotiation of key contracts to merely sending someone a copy of a circular.

Subordinates

The numbers and levels of any jobs reporting to the postholder should be recorded, although this information should also be available as part of any organization chart forming part of the job description.

Dimensions

Any financial or statistical data relevant to the job should be included, as this helps to give a good indication of job size. It is particularly useful for evaluation purposes and when developing performance measures or for reviewing jobs and structures.

Working conditions

Where there are special working conditions applying to the job, eg work in a noisy, hazardous or dirty environment, this should be recorded on the job description.

Knowledge, skills and experience

While the knowledge, qualifications, skills and experience required to do the job are strictly part of a personnel specification rather than a job description, it is useful to include them on one composite document which can then be used for a variety of purposes. This should refer to what is required for full and effective performance of the job, not necessarily what the postholder actually has.

Competencies

Competencies are the personal characteristics and qualities of individuals that enable them to perform their jobs effectively. They can take the form of deep-seated traits or easily observed skills and behaviours. The key is that they are described in such a way that they become observable and measurable.

Other information

There are various miscellaneous pieces of information which it is useful to include on any job description. This might include, for example, any *ex officio* posts normally associated with the job but which are not regarded as an essential part of it for most purposes.

Signatures and date

Any job description should be signed by both the postholder and his or her direct line manager to indicate that it is an agreed document and, in view of how quickly such documents can become out of date, the date of its completion is an important piece of information.

Activity — Preparing a job description

1. Look at your job description, if you have one, and those of colleagues in the organization. Do they describe the outputs you (and they) have to achieve or rather do they describe the tasks you carry out, eg write reports, attend meetings, liaise with . . ., etc?

2. Try writing your own job description with the focus on the results you have to achieve and will be held accountable for. Start with the output, which should be desribed in a way that implies some form of measurement, eg 'ensure attainment of all productivity targets', and then describe what you do to achieve that end result, eg 'direct and control the staff of the . . .' etc, and put this in front of the output. You now have an accountability statement. Up to 10 of these should form the core of your job description.

3. Describe the other aspects of your job using the headings outlined in this chapter. In particular try to answer, directly or by implication, the following questions:
   - Who do you report to?
   - Who reports to you?
   - Who are your main contacts and why?
   - What are the most difficult aspects of your job?
   - What would happen, or not happen, if your job did not exist?
   - What cash sums are you responsible for?
   - What decisions can you make?
   - Who else do you depend on to achieve your objectives?
   - What qualifications, skills and experience are required to do your job fully and well?

References

[1] Boyatzis, R E (1982) *The Competent Manager: A Model for Effective Performance*, Wiley-Interscience, New York.

[2] McCormick, E J, Jeanneret, P R and Mecham, R C (1972) 'A study of job characteristics and job dimensions based on the Position Analysis Questionnaire (PAQ)', *Journal of Applied Psychology*, vol 56.

[3] Spencer, L M Jr, McClelland, D C and Spencer, S M (1992) *Competency Assessment Methods: History and State of the Art*, Hay/McBer Research Press.

[4] HR-BC Ltd and Industrial Relations Services (1993) *Competency and the Link to HR Practice — A Survey of Leading Organisations*.

organizations it has very frequently been possible to reduce staff numbers by reorganizing and by increasing the productivity of those remaining. When business is tight this is easier to achieve, as people will be less willing to put their jobs at risk and may consequently be prepared to work harder for lower rewards. However, in the longer term such an approach may lead to resentment on the part of employees.

Flexible working

More flexible working arrangements may be another way of achieving the same productivity without having to increase or maintain staff numbers. These can take many different forms. At the simplest level, increased overtime can compensate for a shortfall in staff numbers, although clearly this lacks a certain degree of flexibility. Flexible working hours and annual hours agreements can be particularly valuable mechanisms for covering longer daytime working hours (eg longer opening hours in shops) or seasonal variations in workload (eg in horticulture). Teleworking can enable people to be highly productive from a home base without having to spend time and money commuting. This is a particularly attractive option for those with family commitments.

Using part-time or casual staff

Rather than employ full-time members of staff it might make sense to employ part-time or possibly casual staff. The difference between the two is that part-time staff are actually employed on a regular basis for a set number of hours, whereas casual staff are hired as and when the need arises. The latter arrangement is obviously a more flexible one but it needs to be remembered that casual staff can acquire the rights of permanent employees in certain circumstances. Whether or not these are reasonable options will of course depend on the nature of the work to be undertaken.

An alternative is to employ agency staff, who are available to cover a range of functions, particularly for secretarial and clerical jobs.

Using contractors

Contractors are commercial providers of services for which the organization has to pay. They are not employees and are not guaranteed work. It makes sense to use contractors whenever the organization has a periodic rather than a permanent need for a particular service. It has frequently been argued by management gurus that organizations should 'stick to their knitting' and not try to provide services they know little about. For this reason it normally makes more sense to buy in non-core services, such as legal advice, rather than try to provide it in-house. Contracting out of services is an increasing trend in the public sector where there is continuing pressure to reduce costs.

Also an increasing trend is the employment of what are known as interim executives. These are experienced executives who will generally have senior-level experience of an area which they may be brought in to cover. This means that they can be employed for a period of months to cover for short-term absences or to cope with peak workloads and that, because they are highly experienced people, they will be able to 'hit the ground running', requiring a minimum of induction or training.

Staff transfer or promotion

The possibility of transferring an employee into a vacancy should always be considered because not only might it resolve the problem, but it could also provide useful development for the individual transferred. Similarly, there is always the question of whether a post can be filled by internal promotion rather than by seeking to fill it from outside the organization. This can have obvious benefits from the point of view of motivation and morale.

Job sharing

Job sharing is another practice that has become more common in recent years and that has some obvious benefits for those with other commitments. It can open jobs to people who might not otherwise have been able to consider applying.

Computerization

The benefits of savings from the computerization of work have long been claimed but in the past the only results have seemed to be increased staff numbers and substantial IT functions. The main reason for this seems to have been that the past emphasis has been on producing ever more information rather than trying to reduce staff effort. However, we now appear to be entering an era when the long-promised productivity savings are beginning to materialize. Certainly wherever large-scale number processing takes place consideration should be given to whether computerization could reduce effort and staff costs.

IDENTIFYING THE JOB REQUIREMENTS

This stage of the process entails being clear about the content of the job, and the characteristics required of the person in order to perform the job to the necessary standard. This means that there should first be a clear job description — and the need to fill a vacancy is an ideal opportunity to review any existing job description to ensure that it still meets the organization's requirements — and a personnel specification setting out the characteristics required of the jobholder. The preparation of job descriptions is considered in more detail in Chapter 3. Not only will these documents assist in selection but they will also reduce the risk of discrimination in the process.

Content of the personnel or person specification

The personnel specification defines the qualifications, skills, knowledge, experience and personal attributes required of the ideal person for the job. While there are a number of ways of describing these, two common systems for drawing them up are Alec Rodger's Seven-Point Plan[1] and Munro Fraser's Five-Fold Grading System (see below).[2]

Seven-Point Plan

1. **Physical make-up** — health, appearance, bearing and speech.
2. **Attainments** — education, qualifications, experience.
3. **General intelligence** — intellectual capacity.
4. **Special aptitudes** — mechanical, manual dexterity, facility in use of words and figures.
5. **Interests** — intellectual, practical, constructional, physically active, social, artistic.
6. **Disposition** — acceptability, influence over others, steadiness, dependability, self-reliance.
7. **Circumstances** — any special demands of the job, such as ability to work unsocial hours, travel abroad, etc.

Five Fold Grading System

1. **Impact on others** — physical make-up, appearance, speech and manner.
2. **Acquired qualifications** — education, vocational training, work experience.
3. **Innate abilities** — quickness of comprehension and aptitude for learning.
4. **Motivation** — individual goals, consistency and determination in following them up, success rate.
5. **Adjustment** — emotional stability, ability to stand up to stress and ability to get on with people.

Both these approaches can be used as checklists during selection interviews and their use does lend some structure to the process. However, there can be a tendency to mark up those candidates who are preferred for whatever reason. There is, particularly, a tendency for interviewers to wish to recruit people like themselves. This is considered further in the section below on interviewing.

The skill, qualification and experience requirements should be those that are strictly necessary for the effective performance of the job. The inclusion of factors that are unnecessary might unfairly discriminate against minority groups.

Some organizations also specify the behavioural characteristics or competencies required for the jobholder to be effective within the organization's culture. Where competencies are specified there needs to be a framework for identifying them, such as that set out in Figure 4.2 which

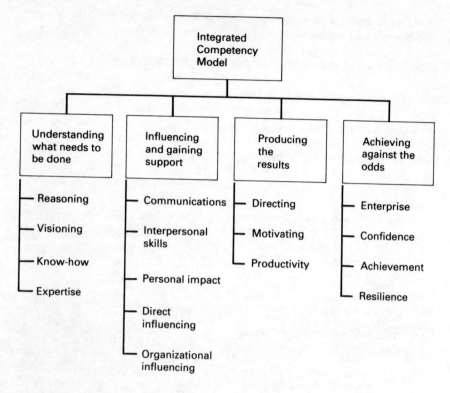

Figure 4.2 *MSL/McBer competencies — themes and clusters*

describes the MSL/McBer competency cluster for managerial jobs. However, the identification of competencies requires approaches that are more sophisticated than the typical selection interview.

Finally, where a new or changed job is being filled, there is likely to be a need to consider the rate of pay or grade and the conditions of employment to be attached to the job. How to determine pay is considered in detail in Chapter 8.

RECRUITMENT SOURCES

There are a number of potential sources of candidates for jobs[3].

The organization itself

The first port of call when considering how to fill a vacancy will usually be the organization itself and this can have advantages in terms of motivation, morale and development, as discussed above. On the other hand, too much internal recruitment can starve the organization of fresh ideas and approaches from external candidates, so a balance has to be struck. When filling posts from within the organization the key is probably to have a selection process that is perceived by everyone to be fair, otherwise there might be suspicion about the appointments made.

Thought also needs to be given to how the vacancy is to be advertised internally. Noticeboards, for example, are often not read by staff. Internal advertising does have the advantages of speed and low costs.

Word of mouth

Jobs may often be filled by existing employees letting their friends and acquaintances know of any vacancies. While this approach will save the costs of advertising or recruiting by some other means, it can be seen as discriminatory, and there have been court cases that have found this to be the case. The reason is that appointing friends and relatives of existing employees can clearly have the effect of restricting employment opportunities to certain groups only.

There is also the danger that closely knit groups may be formed, which while they may have a great deal of loyalty to the organization, may become exclusive cliques or be perceived as such by others in the organization. Such groups might form their own norms and undermine the overall loyalty of the majority of employees.

Newspaper and magazine advertisements

A common way of advertising is through local or national newspapers or professional journals and magazines. The most appropriate medium will depend on the job being filled and on the advertising budget. Local newspapers are more appropriate for jobs to which applicants will probably be recruited locally, eg clerical or manual posts, and where there is a local pool of suitable labour. For senior posts the market is more likely to be a national one, justifying the use of a national newspaper, although this is likely to prove costly.

For particular types of specialist and professional posts professional journals may be appropriate. These have the advantage that they reach exactly the group the advertisement is aimed at and can therefore produce a high response rate even though the circulation is substantially less than that of a newspaper.

Jobcentres and employment agencies

Department of Employment Jobcentres will display job vacancies and refer possible recruits to an organization. Agencies tend to specialize in one particular type of staff such as secretaries or accountants.

Whereas the service provided by Jobcentres is free, agencies charge a fee if an appointment is made. On the other hand, specialist agencies are more likely to be able to provide a good match with the employer's requirements and will have a better understanding of particular occupations. In practice, however, the sheer proliferation of agencies means that some of them are not as professional as they could be and can prove frustrating to the employer by sending along applicants who are clearly unsuitable.

Selection consultants

One of the main advantages of using selection consultants is that they can bring considerable expertise to the selection process and can frequently give advice on the kinds of reward and benefits package that is likely to attract suitable candidates. They can take many aspects of the process out of the hands of the employer including, for example, advertising vacancies, interviewing and shortlisting candidates and providing assistance with the final selection. They can also allow the employer to remain anonymous, if desired.

The greatest drawback is probably cost, fees usually being based on a percentage of salary and ranging from about 10 to 25 per cent. The service will usually be provided on a no result-no fee basis and it may also be possible to recoup the fee if the candidate leaves within a certain period. Some take the view that the use of selection consultants sends a message to internal staff that there is no suitable internal candidate, whereas the reality may be that the organization wants to be seen to be scrupulously fair about the process. Where an internal candidate is appointed to a post through the use of an external consultant, it is likely to strengthen the credibility of that candidate.

Executive search consultants (headhunters)

This approach is more appropriate for the most senior vacancies where the organization has a very specific requirement. In this case the consultants will conduct a market search, often targeting people in senior positions in other organizations or referring to their own database of candidates. This is a very useful way of approaching individuals who are known to be suitable, but without revealing the name of the organization.

The main drawbacks are that it can be costly and will automatically exclude those outside the headhunter's network, who may nevertheless be very able but with a low profile. One other possible drawback is that there is an assumption that those who are currently occupying comparable positions would be suitable candidates, but this takes no account of how well they might be performing in those positions.

Schools and universities

Maintaining regular contact with schools, colleges and the local careers advisory service can help to provide a flow of potential employees. In this way the organization can recruit those with appropriate qualifications who can then be suitably trained. This approach might also help to enhance the local reputation of the employer. Recruitment by visiting universities, the 'milk round', can again provide a pool of applicants with suitable qualifications.

However, this can involve substantial numbers of interviews with those who are really just seeking information rather than a definite job.

Both these approaches are relatively low in cost. However, the main drawback is that they do not provide access to people with any significant amount of work experience.

DRAWING UP AN ADVERTISEMENT

When drawing up an advertisement the following rules should be followed:

1. Consider the key aspects of the job and ensure that these are appropriately stressed.
2. Describe the organization and a few key features.
3. State the job title and summarize the main duties or accountabilities.
4. Describe the location.
5. Summarize the salary and main benefits (failure to reveal the salary will usually reduce the number of applicants).
6. Describe the main characteristics required of the successful applicant, normally those contained in the personnel specification.
7. Describe the method of application and any closing date.
8. Adapt the style of the advertisement to the type of job being filled.
9. Ensure that no aspect of the advertisement is discriminatory.
10. Ensure that the advertisement attracts attention, stimulates and maintains interest, and encourages action.
11. Bear in mind that this is an opportunity to market the organization and to sell the benefits of the job.

There are a number of advertising agencies that will help with the design and placing of advertisements to ensure the maximum response.

Advertisements can be used to invite enquiries following which further information about the job will be provided. BBC Engineering Recruitment uses an approach in which the initial enquiry results in the applicant being provided with full information about the job and selection processes plus a self-selection guide which provides further information about the more demanding aspects of the job, samples of the assessment tests used and application documents. This enables the candidate to make a realistic self-assessment which improves the quality of applications submitted[4].

The organization should be clear about how it is going to handle responses, in particular whether individuals are to be given information packs or are to be invited to telephone for further information. There needs to be a process in place for handling applications as they come in. These should always be acknowledged (unless, as happens in some cases, applicants are told in advance that there will be no acknowledgement because of the volumes involved). Failure to do so, which happens all too often, gives the organization a bad image. The responses to advertisements should also be monitored to determine which formats and media produce the best responses.

Activity — Job advertisements

Review a job advertisement in a newspaper or magazine. You may wish to consider the following questions among others:

1. Did it catch your attention?
2. Did it look interesting?
3. Will it attract the right applicants?
4. Was it worded in a personal or an impersonal way?
5. Did it give answers to basic questions such as where the job is located, whether you could do it, the likely level of reward, etc?
6. Did it give a good impression of the organization?

SELECTION METHODS

Application form or Curriculum Vitae?

The selection process really begins with the organization's choice of how the applicant should respond to an advertisement (if that is the preferred route), ie whether it should be by application form, a letter of application/ curriculum vitae (CV) or by telephone. The method chosen will often be determined by the seniority of the job and the anticipated number of replies. The CV is more commonly used for very senior jobs and experience shows that asking for application forms for such posts will reduce the number of applicants. The initial sifting of candidates' suitability for a particular job begins with this decision.

Application forms   — example of app form.

The advantages and disadvantages of using an application form are set out in Table 4.1.

Application forms are used extensively by a wide variety of organizations and can help to achieve cost-effective recruitment. In a recent study[5] Industrial Relations Services gave examples of a number of organizations where extensive and effective use was made of forms. These included the Employment Service which recruits about 3000 staff a year, and Bosch which had to recruit 700 staff in one go to a new factory in Cardiff. For Bosch a newly designed application form played a crucial part in helping to sift through the 10,000 or so applications.

Letters of application/CVs

The main alternative approach is to invite a letter of application or ask for a CV. The advantages and disadvantages are explained in Table 4.2.

Telephone

Inviting applications by telephone can produce a rapid response to an advertisement and can cut out much of the bureaucracy surrounding more

Table 4.1 *Advantages and disadvantages of application forms*

Advantages	Disadvantages
As information is structured it is easier to compare candidates.	Different forms may have to be prepared for different jobs.
The organization gets the information it wants.	There is little opportunity for the candidate to display creative flair.
The form can be used as the basis for the interview.	Insufficient space is sometimes provided and additional pages have to be attached.
Some applicants prefer forms.	Forms put some people off.
Standard of completion gives an indication of a candidate's suitability.	Badly designed forms could cause difficulties.
It can form part of the personnel file.	
It reduces the likelihood of unfairness or discrimination.	
Forms can be used to collect data for equal opportunities and research purposes.	
Information can more easily be computerized.	
Forms can reinforce positive messages about the organization.	

traditional approaches. Some rapid screening can be carried out to determine whether the process should be taken any further and this can clearly save time and effort for both the organization and the applicant. To ensure that the process works effectively it is best to use some type of telephone screening form.

Table 4.2 *Advantages and disadvantages of letters of application and CVs*

Advantages	Disadvantages
The standard of presentation will give some idea of the suitability of the applicant, although there are a number of companies who will prepare a professional CV for a fee.	The fact that they can be professionally produced can give a misleading impression of the applicant's narrative skills.
There is no danger that the applicant will be discouraged by having to complete an application form.	The greater variability in the type and format of information provided make like for like comparisons more difficult
Different aspects of background and experience can be covered as fully as the individual thinks fit.	The applicant will give the information that he or she wants to give, not necessarily what the organization wants.
Individuals can prepare a standard CV that can be sent out very quickly.	

Interviews

A selection interview is a controlled conversation between an applicant for a job and the employer, or someone representing the employer, designed to test the suitability of the applicant for the job in question. It is a two-way exchange of information designed to help the interviewer form an opinion about the candidate and the candidate about the organization. In the selection process the specific aims of the interviewer are:

- to find out as much job-relevant information as possible about the applicant so that his or her suitability for the job can be assessed against the pre-determined criteria for effective job performance;
- to give further information about the job and the organization;
- to ensure that the process is as fair as possible and is perceived to be fair.

The interview remains one of the most common and popular ways of selecting staff even though it has been subjected to a number of criticisms. The most common of these criticisms, which are supported by research findings, are as follows:

- Interviewers make up their mind about a candidate within the first three or four minutes of the interview and spend the rest of the interview looking for evidence to confirm their original view.
- Interviews seldom change the opinion formed from the original application and the candidate's appearance.
- There is a tendency to give more weight to unfavourable evidence than to that which is favourable.
- When interviewers make up their minds early in the interview their behaviour tends to convey this to the candidate.
- One overriding characteristic, such as appearance or speech, can tend to overshadow other factors.
- Where there are a number of interviewers there is frequently disagreement between them about candidates, sometimes leaving the way open for everyone's second choice.
- Interviewers tend to recruit in their own likeness.

Despite these drawbacks the interview remains popular because:

- it is perhaps the best way to assess the compatibility of the candidate with his or her colleagues or boss, which is probably one of the most crucial factors affecting the success of any employment relationship;
- it is a flexible and quick way of gaining information about a candidate and of giving more information about the job and the organization;
- as Torrington and Hall have identified,[6] there is also a ritualistic aspect to the interview — it is usually an expected and accepted part of the process.

Some recent research[7] with 60 selection interviewers and 90 candidates has shown that interviewing is perceived by the majority of interviewers

(95 per cent in this example) and candidates (85 per cent in this example) as a fair method of selection. In Italy, little use is made of any other form of selection.

Interviews can take a number of different forms. They may be formal or informal, be conducted by one individual or by several, or follow one of a number of strategies or techniques. Often, particularly where more senior jobs are concerned, a number of interviews might be involved, each with a different format.

In parts of the public sector, local authorities for example, there will frequently be an initial informal interview with one or two individuals, often the line manager of the job in question and a representative of the personnel function, followed by a formal interview by committee. Very often the preliminary interview focuses on the more technical aspects of the job with the more formal one paying more attention to the individual and to the fit between the individual and the job. However, there are no hard and fast rules about this and many different combinations are possible.

One of the problems with panel or committee interviews, apart from the potential for disagreement noted earlier, is that more junior members of the panel may feel constrained to take the same line as the boss. There is also a likelihood that they will tend to err on the side of caution and go for the safe bet rather than the human dynamo.

Group interviews are sometimes used in which several potential candidates are interviewed together. This involves group discussions usually supplemented by tests. This is perhaps more appropriate in highly competitive environments and where there are a number of posts to be filled. However, it can be a daunting prospect for the candidates concerned.

Conducting successful interviews

There are a number of rules to be followed when conducting selection interviews. These are as follows.

Before the interview

1. Ensure that candidates are adequately briefed about the organization and the job (although you may wish to test their knowledge of both).
2. Ensure that you prepare for the interview by reading through the relevant applications and have available all necessary documentation including the job description and the personnel specification.
3. Arrange a venue that is free from interruption and, if necessary, have telephone calls diverted.
4. Ensure that you, any other interviewers and the candidates know the time, date and venue.
5. Ensure that enough time is set aside for the interviews and allow time for discussing applicants and for any possible overrun.
6. Formulate some questions in advance and ensure that all important aspects are covered.

7. Where more than one interviewer is involved, decide who will chair the interview and who will ask what questions.
8. Try to ensure that all those involved in interviewing have been trained in the process.
9. Give some thought to the seating arrangements and to the kind of interview you wish to conduct — sitting on sofas around a coffee table gives a very different impression to that conveyed by a row of interviewers behind a desk.
10. Make appropriate arrangements for the reception of applicants, in particular giving them somewhere to sit, ensuring that they are told where the cloakroom facilities are (a small point, but an important one) and making sure that the reception staff know they are coming.

During the interview

1. Try to stick to the timetable — it seems often to be the norm that interviews overrun. That is both bad planning and bad manners, as candidates presumably have other commitments as well.
2. Follow a clear structure during the interview so that there is an obvious beginning, middle and end.
3. Start by welcoming the candidate and try to put him or her at ease, perhaps by chatting about something inconsequential.
4. Introduce yourself and any other interviewers.
5. State the purpose of the interview and describe how it is to be conducted.
6. Try to ask questions that are open ended and encourage discussion — basically questions that begin with who? what? where? when? why? and how? or phrases such as 'tell us what you think about ...'
7. Ensure that you avoid questions that could be construed as discriminatory.
8. Avoid just going back over the application form repeating the information that is already there — a common fault. However, clarify anything that is not clear.
9. Do not hesitate to probe if the need arises — it is better to get any doubts out into the open than to wonder about them afterwards.
10. Listen carefully to the replies, remembering that most of the talking should be done by the candidate, and try to read between the lines.
11. Ask the interviewee to supply examples of the kinds of things he or she has done to get a clear idea of current and past experience.
12. Keep notes of what is said, and if a number of candidates are being interviewed it is a good idea, in the absence of a photograph, to write a short pen-portrait of each of them — it is surprisingly easy to get confused after interviewing, say, six people in one day.
13. At the end of the interview invite the candidate to ask any questions about the job or the organization.
14. Tell the candidate when to expect to hear the outcome.

After the interview

1. Discuss and record your conclusion.
2. Notify the candidates of the outcome as soon as possible — you may wish to delay telling any reserve candidate until the first choice has accepted but this delay should not be too long.
3. Negotiate the salary and terms of employment with the successful candidate and prepare a contract of employment.
4. Undertake follow-up research through interview or by using the organization's performance management process to check whether the selection predictions have proved accurate.

Selection tests

The defects of the more traditional methods of recruitment have led many organizations to look for more objective predictors of performance. There are a variety of tests designed to do this, and the main ones are described briefly below.

Psychometric tests

Psychometric tests involve applying standard procedures to applicants in such a way that their responses can be quantified, thereby enabling objective comparisons to be made. Such tests should satisfy six criteria. Any test should be:

1. A sensitive measuring instrument that discriminates between subjects.
2. Standardized, so that an individual score can be related to others.
3. Reliable, in that it always measures the same thing.
4. Valid, in that the test measures what it is designed to measure.
5. Acceptable to the candidate.
6. Non-discriminatory.

There are a number of different types of psychometric test which, for selection purposes, may be classified as intelligence tests, aptitude and attainment tests, and personality tests.

Intelligence tests

Intelligence tests are the oldest kind of psychometric test, having been designed by Binet and Simon in 1905. They are rarely, if ever, used for selection purposes these days. The scores are expressed in terms of the Intelligence Quotient or IQ which is the ratio of mental age to the chronological age of the individual. As intelligence is assumed to follow a normal distribution throughout the population, there will be approximately even numbers of people above and below the mid-point or mean. The mean is scored as 100 and all other scores are related to this figure.

The main problem with intelligence tests is that they are attempting to measure something which is very complex and about which there is much disagreement. It is possible that intelligence tests only measure an ability to do intelligence tests. In any case, they have limited application in the selection context and their use in the wrong circumstances could provoke resentment if candidates feel that they have already proved their intellectual capacity through their qualifications and experience.

Aptitude and attainment tests

These tests are designed to test particular aptitudes or abilities and can therefore be made very relevant to the job in question. Aptitude tests measure an individual's potential to develop, whereas attainment tests measure skills that have already been acquired. Aptitude tests can examine such things as verbal and numerical reasoning skills, spatial ability, manual dexterity, etc. Some of the most common attainment tests are typing tests, which are widely used and accepted. The most important aspect in designing all such tests is to ensure that they are properly validated.

Personality tests

Personality is an even vaguer word than intelligence and this is probably the biggest problem with personality tests. What exactly are they measuring? There are a number of different theories about personality and a number of different definitions. Heim[8] has even stated that a theory of personality is not practicable. However, one definition[9] that seems to contain most of the agreed elements is as follows:

> Personality is the integration of all of an individual's characteristics into a unique organization that determines, and is modified by, his attempts at adaptation to his continually changing environment.

Personality tests can take a number of different forms, testing, for example, individual traits or characteristics, interests, or values. Others may concentrate on specific workplace behaviour.

Some of the more common tests include the 16PF, Myers-Briggs, the FIRO-B and Saville and Holdsworth's OPQ. There has been much debate about the validity of personality tests and studies have given variable results, but they are generally found to be more valid than the standard interview, especially when used in combination with other techniques. Studies by Schmitt and Gooding[10] and Barrick and Mount,[11] in particular, have strongly supported their validity.

Using tests

Whatever tests are used, they should:

■ ideally, be used as part of and integrated with the selection procedure and supported by other approaches;

■   be rigorously designed and validated;

■   be administered by or supported by advice from someone trained to the standards of the British Psychological Society.

Companies like ICL and Barclays Bank which make extensive use of psychometric tests ensure that they are rigorously controlled and administered only by fully trained and qualified users.

The use of psychometric tests tends to be less widespread in Europe generally, with even a company as large as Mercedes-Benz not using either tests or assessment centres (see below).

Assessment centres

An assessment centre is a planned programme of tests, exercises and group selection techniques designed to assess the suitability of participants for promotion in general or for a particular job. Despite the name it is not something that is necessarily held in one place. An example of an assessment centre approach is given in the following case study.

Case Study — Recruitment of a chief executive in a local authority

The council members of a district council wished to recruit a new chief executive and in view of the importance of the position felt that a significant investment of their time and effort was justified. They therefore engaged an external consultancy to assist with the design of an assessment centre to select a suitable person. The selection process involved the following elements:

1. Initial sifting of applications from advertisements placed in national newspapers and local goverment journals.
2. A two-stage technical interview to select a shortlist of six or so potential candidates.
3. A two-day assessment centre for the shortlisted candidates, involving:
   - ■ a tour of some of the council's major projects and facilities, escorted by members, senior council officers and a consultant, solely to impart information to the candidates;
   - ■ a battery of psychometric tests;
   - ■ a presentation from each candidate;
   - ■ a structured discussion;
   - ■ interviews by a committee of members;
   - ■ an in-tray exercise based on research about the problems actually dealt with by a typical district council chief executive.

In the event, while the results of the psychometric tests were important, more weight was attached by the selection panel of council members to the in-tray exercise and, particularly, to the interviews. As always, getting the right match in the interpersonal relationships was probably the crucial factor. The council also had a very clear perception of the type of psychological make-up it was looking for.

Was the effort worth the return? It is now some time since the appointment was made and the general view is that they got it right.

LIVERPOOL JOHN MOORES UNIVERSITY
LEARNING SERVICES

Assessment centres can also be used for management development when they are usually described as development centres. The main aim is to give information to the organization about individual competencies which can then be developed to suit the organization. A range of tests are used and in this way performance can be measured along several dimensions, as can the interactions among the candidates. Tests such as in-tray exercises may be used to supplement group exercises.

Bio data

Bio data selection involves selection on the basis of biographical information including age, qualifications and jobs held. It is based on the assumption that past experience and attainments are likely to be a good predictor of job performance. Bio data questionnaires vary in the number and types of question asked but will typically seek such information as number of jobs, length of employment, hobbies and interests, etc. Their main drawbacks are that they can be discriminatory because of the nature of the questions asked, they need to be individually designed for different organizations, and they can quickly become out of date.

Graphology

Graphology — analysing character from handwriting — is only used to any significant degree in France and French-speaking companies in Belgium. Elsewhere it is not generally regarded as an accurate or valid method of selection.

Random selection

Many organizations receive huge numbers of applications — often several thousand — for jobs and sifting through these to shortlist suitable applicants can be very taxing on selectors who have to find some way of coping with the volume. This can sometimes lead to the arbitrary selection of irrelevant criteria to exclude certain people. This can undermine the selection process and could lead to discrimination. To get round this problem some organizations have turned to random selection of applicants with the aid of a computer, the logic being that in this way everyone has an equal chance of being selected.

Effectiveness of selection methods

There have been numerous studies on the effectiveness of various selection methods, although these measurements are often difficult to make, partly because of the complexity of assessing performance in jobs. However, a relatively reliable method of analysis, known as meta-analysis, which reviews the results of numerous samples, a kind of study of studies, gives the results set out in Figure 4.3.

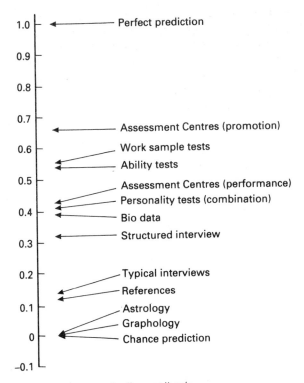

Figure 4.3 *Accuracy of some selection methods*
Source: MSL Human Resource Consultants

Taking up references

The purpose of a reference is to gain information about an individual from a source who knows the person's capabilities well enough to be able to comment on them, and to assess the individual's suitability for the job in question. The reference should seek both factual information about previous experience, for example, and also character information.

The usual source of such information is the applicant's previous employer and this is likely to be the best source for gaining information about working ability and attitude. Personal references from friends are a waste of time.

References may be taken up at any stage of the selection process, although in the public sector it tends to be before the final interview, whereas in the private sector confidentiality is preserved until an offer is made. Any appointment made should be subject to the receipt of satisfactory references. The permission of the applicant should always be obtained before taking up references.

The key information the prospective employer should seek from any previous employer includes:

- How long the applicant was employed.
- The job that was undertaken.
- The salary or wage paid.
- The number of days' absence.
- How satisfied the employer was with the applicant's performance.
- Whether re-employment would be considered and if not, why not.

While references are usually obtained by writing to the referee there is considerable merit in getting a telephone reference. The reason for this is that people will often reveal things over the telephone that they might be reluctant to put in writing. It is also often the case that the tone of voice will tell a great deal about the previous employer's attitude to the candidate.

It should also be borne in mind that while obtaining references should be regarded as an essential part of the selection process, they are not entirely reliable. The previous employer might have held an unreasonable grudge against the applicant, or as can sometimes happen the reference can be so glowing as to make the recipient wonder if the writer is anxious to lose the individual concerned. In such cases a telephone call is almost essential. The employer should, in any case, obtain more than one reference and compare the results.

References

[1] Rodger, A (1952) *The Seven Point Plan*, NIIP, London.

[2] Munro Fraser, J (1954) *Handbook of Employment Interviewing*, Macdonald and Evans, London.

[3] ACAS Advisory Booklet No. 6, *Recruitment and Selection*, revised 1984.

[4] Schofield, P (1993) 'Improving the candidate-job match', *Personnel Management*, February.

[5] 'Ensuring effective recruitment: developments in the use of application forms and random selection', *Industrial Relations Review and Report* No. 556, March 1994.

[6] Torrington, D and Hall, L (1991) *Personnel Management: A New Approach*, 2nd edn, Prentice Hall, Hemel Hempstead.

[7] Fletcher, C (1992) 'Ethics and the job interview', *Personnel Management*, March.

[8] Heim, A (1975) *Intelligence and Personality*, Penguin Books, Harmondsworth.

[9] Krech, D, Crutchfield, R S and Livson, N (1969) *Elements of Psychology*, Knopf, New York.

[10] Schmitt, N, Gooding, R Z, Noe, R A and Kirsch, M (1984) 'Meta-analysis of validity studies published between 1964 and 1982 and the investigation of study characteristics', *Personnel Psychology* 37.

[11] Barrick, M R and Mount, M K (1991) 'The big five personality dimensions and job performance: a meta-analysis', *Personnel Psychology*, 44.

5

Managing Performance

The theme of this chapter is the management of individual performance in the organization. Although the emphasis is on the individual, it is important to bear in mind that the effectiveness of people's performance is dependent on the organization itself having a clear mission, strategy and objectives. Provided the overall direction is clear, it is then possible to specify the outputs to be achieved by the individual components of the organization, including departments, sections, individuals, and the processes necessary to achieve those outputs. Without this clarity those same individuals, departments etc will be charging off in all directions without any particular destination in sight. This context is summarized in Figure 5.1.

The organization's mission or purpose will set out the reason for its existence and establish the point it ultimately wants to reach. The mission itself should normally be broken down into a number of more discrete goals which form the basis of the organization's overall strategy or policy. The strategy in turn will specify objectives for the various components of the organization, which should be both quantitative and qualitative in nature. While the goals may be general statements of ambition or intent, objectives have to be much more specific and be, as far as possible, measurable.

In similar vein, jobs are created for particular reasons and to achieve specific outputs. While these outputs may often be difficult to measure, there should nevertheless be clear statements of accountability as far as these can be determined. These accountabilities will enable managers to determine what specific targets each postholder has to attain and to encourage the development of action plans.

The effective management of performance is probably one of the biggest problems now facing organizations. The modern organization has to be lean, efficient and have relatively few levels in the hierarchy to survive and thrive. The consequence of reduced staff numbers is that those who remain are required to perform that much more effectively. Effective performance for the organization means that output can be maintained with fewer numbers or productivity increased.

Performing effectively is also of crucial importance to people. While at

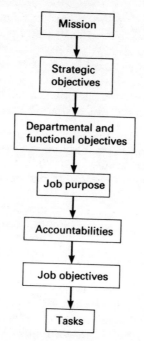

Figure 5.1 *The job in the context of organizational objectives*

one time it was relatively easy to remain in employment with mediocre performance, provided any drastic breaches of discipline were avoided, this is no longer the case. Because organizations (with certain exceptions) can no longer tolerate poor performance, people are more likely to be dismissed. Those people then have to compete with numerous others in the search for work. The effective management of performance, therefore, is not only vital for the long-term survival of the organization but is also a moral obligation on the employer as it is clearly in the best interests of the employee.

There is really no choice between managing performance and not doing so. It is the most important role of the manager, since without it the organization will simply be a collection of activities with no particular focus or control.

DEFINING PERFORMANCE MANAGEMENT

There are a number of different definitions of performance management, but our preference is:

A management process designed to link the organization's objectives with those of the individual in such a way as to ensure that both individual and corporate objectives are, as far as possible, met.

There is an underlying assumption in this that if individuals can satisfy their own needs by meeting their objectives and at the same time contribute to the attainment of the organization's objectives, then they are likely to be more highly motivated and achieve greater job satisfaction. This assumption is also at the core of strategic HRM.

In considering the meaning of performance management, it is probably also as well to clarify what it is not. It is not:

1. *Performance appraisal* — invariably when managers in organizations are asked about their performance management process, they describe their performance appraisal system. While the performance appraisal interview is probably an inescapable part of a performance management process, it is only a *part* of it.

2. *Performance related pay* — while cash and other rewards may very well be part of a performance management process, it is vitally important that they are considered as a separate issue.

3. *Something done by the personnel manager* — there is often a tendency to regard performance management solely as a technique of human resource management, usually because that is the department that initiates the process, monitors the standards and maintains the personnel records. In fact, to be successful it is a process that has to be owned by the directors and managers of the organization.

4. *A magic bullet* — performance management is not the answer to all the organization's problems. It is only one of a number of systems that must be used effectively in any organization if it is to achieve short- and long-term success.

5. *An objective-setting process* — again, while setting objectives is a crucial part of performance management, it is only part of it. Setting objectives and then leaving people to strive to attain them without giving support in the form of training, resources, encouragement, commitment and effective management is unlikely to achieve the desired results.

6. *A fashion or fad* — in any organization judgements are made about the way people perform and how certain outputs are produced. The issue is really whether those judgements are based on sound and objective evaluations, whether the outputs are the ones that are desired and whether they are quantitatively and qualitatively at the right level.

FEATURES OF A SUCCESSFUL PERFORMANCE MANAGEMENT PROCESS

A performance management process that is operating effectively should produce the following results:

- Clear objectives for the organization and a sound process for identifying, developing, measuring and reviewing them.
- An integration of corporate objectives set by senior management with the aims of individual employees.

- Greater clarity about the organization's aspirations and objectives.
- The development of a 'performance culture' in which results are given a greater priority than the more cosmetic aspects of organizational functioning such as conforming to standard procedures.
- The establishment of a continuing dialogue between management and employees and a consequently greater emphasis on individual development needs.
- The development of a more open and learning environment in which ideas and solutions are put forward and discussed in a non-judgemental way and with the consequent development of a learning culture.
- An organization which makes things happen and achieves results.
- Encouragement for self-development.

While the above outcomes may seem like a counsel of perfection and will not all be achievable to the optimum level, they are areas in which tangible improvements are likely to be achieved if the process is properly implemented.

THE PERFORMANCE MANAGEMENT PROCESS

This section described the main stages in the introduction of a comprehensive performance management process. There are four main stages:

1. Planning performance.
2. Managing performance.
3. Reviewing performance.
4. Rewarding performance.

These processes are summarized in Figure 5.2.

Planning performance

As with the introduction of any process, there first needs to be clarity about the primary reason for introducing performance management and a clear view about what it is expected to deliver in terms of results. There also needs to be strong commitment from the top to the introduction of the process, as without this commitment it will be difficult to gain support from the lower echelons of the organization and insufficient resources may be allocated to achieve the desired results.

The next logical step in designing a performance management process is the setting of objectives. Typically, these will derive from the organization's overall direction and strategy, and from broad statements of intent which will be gradually refined, cascading down the organization, until they are translated into individual targets. This is known as the top-down approach. An alternative to this is the bottom-up approach. In this case, as the name suggests, priorities and targets would be identified by those lower down in the organization. In some respects this might seem illogical as it runs

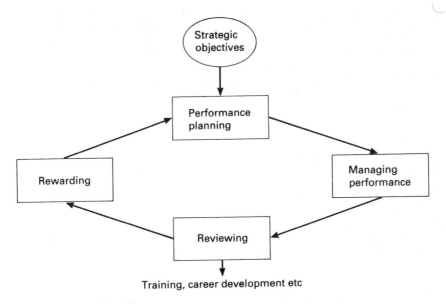

Figure 5.2 *The performance management cycle*

Source: Adapted from Hay

counter to the theory that jobs exist for a particular purpose, and that purpose is determined by the organization's management. Certainly in most situations it would be expected that the targets of individual employees would be dependent on the overall objectives of the organization. However, there are circumstances in which the bottom-up approach can be a useful means of determining overall objectives. This will normally arise in large organizations in which senior management may be a long way removed from the customer or client base. In such circumstances the employees at the 'coal-face' may well have a sounder appreciation of the needs of those customers and/or clients and be therefore better able to decide on the kinds of priorities that are likely to result in greater customer satisfaction.

When consideration is given to target setting for individuals, it should also be borne in mind that those individuals will have aims that are not just work related. Indeed, their priorities are much more likely to revolve around such issues as promotion prospects, pay, recognition, time off, lifestyle, relations with colleagues and the boss.

Objective setting

An objective may be defined as 'a clear statement indicating how a particular output will be achieved in both quantitative and qualitative terms'. Good objectives should conform to what have been described as 'SMART' criteria. That is, they should be:

■ **Sp**ecific — as precise as possible and relating to only one identifiable output.

- **Measurable** — or it will be difficult, if not impossible, to judge when they have been achieved.
- **Achievable** — or they will lose credibility, be demoralizing and serve no useful purpose.
- **Results orientated** — be related to the end result which is to be achieved.
- **Time related** — objectives without a clear timescale give no guidance on priorities.

There are a number of other factors to be taken into account when setting objectives. It has already been stated that they should be achievable, but it should also be borne in mind that the extent to which someone will be motivated to achieve a particular objective will depend on the extent to which they are able to influence it.

In a manufacturing environment, for example, an individual may well have a high degree of control over the number of units produced. Similarly, sales representatives will usually have a high degree of control over the number of visits they might make to potential customers. In these cases objectives can be set which can contain, among other things, certain target volumes to be achieved, and the individuals will usually regard these as being logical, although they might debate the actual numbers selected.

On the other hand, setting targets over which a person has little control will be demoralizing and will be unlikely to result in the set target being reached. There are numerous examples of this. Supervisors may often be held accountable (and should be held accountable) for the motivation and morale of the employees under their control. However, this motivation and morale can suffer for reasons that are totally beyond the control of the supervisor, such as poor business performance, weak senior management, redundancies, etc.

While it is crucial that objectives and targets should be those that individuals can influence, it is also important that they are significant ones for the organization. Almost anyone who works in an office, for example, has a considerable amount of influence over the way in which they organize their paperwork, but setting targets for them to attain in this area is hardly likely to make a significant contribution to the organization (unless that is the organization's business, such as a company which processes credit card transactions on behalf of Barclaycard or American Express). The overriding consideration is that any objectives should, as far as possible, both give the organization some kind of competitive advantage or have an impact on the direction and performance of the business, and also be those over which the individual has a high degree of control. The higher the degree of individual control and the more significant the attainment of a specific objective, the more desirable it is for the organization.

It is very important to ensure that any objectives set relate to corporate objectives and that they align well with those set for other posts. For this reason, objective setting should not be done in isolation for one post only but should take account of all other posts in a particular team or group and of all other individuals and teams with which they interact.

Although objectives have to be achievable, they should also be stretching, to ensure that the organization performs well and grows where possible, and to develop the individual postholder. Objectives that will be attained in any case and with little discernible effort on the part of the postholder are of little value.

Objectives should be set in all the important areas of the job and should not be too numerous, otherwise this will dilute their impact and divert the individual's attention away from the things that really matter. While the precise number will depend on the type of job and the kinds of objectives set, any number significantly greater than ten is likely to be too many for any one person to cope with realistically.

Obviously some objectives will be more important than others and the priorities should be made clear. Those which should be given the greatest priority are the ones which will have the most significant impact on the organization and give the greatest competitive advantage.

A surprisingly difficult aspect of measuring performance is actually knowing when someone has attained his or her targets. Even where clear and concrete measures are available this can still be difficult. For example, if someone is set a sales target of £100,000 in a year but achieves £97,000, is that on target or not? A strict literal interpretation would be that the individual was below target. However, it is more likely that any figures within what may be regarded as an acceptable range would be treated as on-target performance.

It all depends on the circumstances in which the results are obtained and the way in which the performance process operates. What is important is that wherever possible numerical targets are set. Obviously most jobs have certain aspects to them that are not easily measurable and for others the outputs may be very difficult indeed to define. How, for example, can you measure the outputs of a scenes of crime officer in a police force? Or a researcher? In such cases performance objectives may have to relate more to competencies than measurable outputs, and this is considered further below.

Objectives should take into account an individual's personal development. This will be not only in the individual's interest but also the organization's, since a more highly motivated and skilled employee can only be a good thing. Equally, it is by trying to integrate individual aspirations with the aims of the organization that the best results are likely to be obtained.

Once objectives have been set, the manager should ensure that all the necessary support is provided to enable the person to achieve them. There is no point in asking someone to dig a hole if they have not been given a spade. Finally, the overall aim in the performance planning process should be to ensure that people are not only doing things in the right way but, more importantly, that they are focused on the right things.

Activity — Objective setting and performance planning

1. List the main objectives or key results you have to achieve in your job. Make sure that each objective has a clear and measurable performance output and specify a date by which it is to be achieved.
2. List also the information, resources and assistance you will require to meet your objectives.
3. What are the obstacles? How can they be overcome?

Competency based objectives

It has been stated that objectives should, as far as possible, be specific and measurable. This means using clear output measures wherever possible. For many jobs, however, outputs are not at all clear. While generally it is relatively easy to determine performance measures for the most senior management posts in the organization, usually based on overall organization performance and including such parameters as earnings per share, and for the most junior posts, which are likely to be task based (eg number of invoices processed, units produced, calls made), it is much more difficult for those posts in the middle where there is a less direct link with outputs. Similarly, even where there are clear measures, to focus on units of production alone could neglect the qualitative and developmental aspects of any role.

Any performance management scheme should therefore have a mixture of quantifiable outputs and more behaviourally based competencies. The important points in using competencies as performance measures are:

- They must be worded in such a way that they can be objectively assessed, otherwise they run the risk of becoming just a shopping list of desirable traits.
- They must be relevant to the job.
- There should be a common core of competencies for jobs operating in the same environment, otherwise it will be difficult to establish common standards.
- They should not be too numerous otherwise the same thing may be measured more than once[1].

Managing Performance

Once performance objectives have been set and action plans agreed, the next stage of the performance management process is to ensure that those plans are acted on and the required results produced. 'Management' in this sense means much more than conducting an annual appraisal, or even a series of appraisals, although such actions will inevitably form an important part of the process. What it is really about is giving employees the necessary support and creating the appropriate conditions for them to be able to deliver the required results, in effect 'empowering' them. In practical terms this is likely to mean:

- giving any necessary practical support, such as providing the appropriate resources.
- ensuring that employees are clear about the results required and giving any advice or clarification that may be needed.
- giving employees the necessary training and development to ensure that they are able to achieve their accountabilities.
- adjusting targets, priorities and performance measures according to changes in organization priorities, markets, government policies etc.

In essence this involves adopting a management style and approach that help to develop a performance culture in which results are perceived as more important than traditional conventions of behaviour within the organization. For example, there should perhaps be less emphasis on ensuring that people are in the office between certain hours and more on what they produce while they are there, although of course in many environments good timekeeping would be an essential requirement for effective performance.

An important part of managing performance is also taking responsibility for one's own performance. This requirement applies equally to managers and subordinates, but it is particularly important for managers to lead by example.

It is oversimplifying to suggest that there is any one management style that is the best. The most appropriate style in any particular situation will depend on a number of factors, including the personality of the individual, the nature of the task, the timescale and the culture of the organization. For example, in an organization such as the fire service, because the consequences of not acting as a team and responding quickly to direct instructions could be fatal, a directive style of management is most appropriate, at least for operational staff. This is reinforced by strict rules, drills and uniforms. On the other hand, with a team of professional engineers, a more participative style is more appropriate to ensure the fullest consideration of ideas and views and because the nature of the role is to reach agreement through discussion (in most cases). Similarly, some individuals prefer to be directed while others loathe it. Jobs that have to be completed against a very tight deadline require strong direction and control.

Except where tasks are very prescribed, and possibly even then, the most effective management style is likely to be one that empowers individuals to make decisions that are within their competence and that gives them all the necessary support and encouragement. The aim in effectively managing performance, therefore, should be to adopt a style which gives coaching and assists in people's development, but with the option held in reserve of becoming more directive should the need arise. At the end of the day it is the role of the manager to ensure that the results within his or her control are obtained, and delegation or empowerment of subordinates does not absolve the manager of that responsibility. There is a danger that subordinates may not be able to cope with the ambiguity that could arise from the use of different styles at different times. The way round this problem is to make it very clear just what the ground rules are, ie 'the way we do things round here'. Over the years many organizations have written down what their philosophy of management is, as is the case, for example, with the London Borough of Bromley, Grand Metropolitan and Hickson International (see case study).

Case Study — Hickson's basic beliefs and aims

Hickson International sets out a number of basic beliefs including:

- Being a 'leading player' in its chosen markets.
- Placing a high priority on customer satisfaction, quality and service.
- Using 'the best available technology' to develop new products, but also playing a responsible community role, paying proper attention to all safety, health and environmental issues.
- Operating with a lean centre and devolved businesses, working within an agreed strategic framework.
- Encouraging all employees to be innovative, change oriented, adaptable, and able and willing to stretch their performance.

Source: Industrial Relations Review and Report No. 552, January 1994, *A Human Resources Strategy at Hickson International*, Eclipse Group, London.

There has been a lot of emphasis in this chapter on empowering employees and adopting a coaching management style. It is a fact, however, that many employees may not wish to take on responsibility and also that in production environments activities may be so closely defined that such an approach is impractical. Indeed, it has been reported recently that the renowned Volvo production approach, involving group technology and team working, is having to be revised because production costs cannot be kept competitive with more traditional methods.

The ICI approach to performance management has placed a great deal of emphasis on the importance of coaching by line managers. This approach met with some of the traditional objections, prime among which is the amount of time taken up, and how this diverts managers from their real job. This is really rather curious since if it is not the prime role of the manager to ensure optimum performance, just what is? The fact remains that key to the ICI approach, and central to any effective performance management process, is the need to ensure that it is owned by the line managers. What is encouraging about ICI's experience is that even research departments could see the value of objective setting, despite the difficulties.[2]

Reviewing Performance

Strictly speaking, performance review is part of the process of managing performance. However, in view of the specific considerations that apply to this aspect of the process it is convenient to examine it as a separate element.

Where performance appraisal exists, it typically centres round an inter-view held once or twice a year, between the postholder and his or her boss. Sometimes the outcome of this interview can have a direct bearing on pay and promotion, whereas in other cases the emphasis is on training and development. Often performance issues are raised that may not have been discussed at any other time during the year.

Some interviews can be bland, with the employee left with the impression that he or she is performing satisfactorily even though that may not be the manager's true view. This is because a large number of managers find it uncomfortable to be openly critical of their subordinates' performance, even though they may be prepared to make such criticisms to third parties. At the other extreme, interviews can degenerate into sessions for appor-tioning blame for past failures.

What is ideally required is a process that is constructive and supportive and that gives advice that can help the individual improve and develop. Able and well-motivated staff will usually welcome constructive criticism. To achieve this there are certain principles that need to be adhered to:

- The appraisal interview should not contain any surprises. The apprai-see should be well aware of his or her level of performance before the interview because of the regular feedback given by the manager.
- The process should be applied to everybody. Every employee has a right to know how well he or she is doing and it is an obligation on the part of management to let him or her know.
- Employees should be encouraged to review their own performance and give their opinions about how they think they have done.
- The discussion should be focused on the targets that have been set and the achievements against those targets.
- Appraisers should remember the rule that they have two ears and one mouth, to be used in that proportion when conducting the appraisal interview.

Rating performance

A crucial part of performance appraisal is judging how well an individual has performed against identified targets. Generally, assessing results will be easier than judging the quality of those results, but it can be far from straightforward even when the measures seem obvious. In making judge-ments about performance there are a number of key principles to be adhered to:

- The performance should be judged against overall objectives, which may have been broken down into separate targets which together contribute to the overall objective. For example, an objective of reaching a certain level of sales may be comprised of target figures for individual products.
- As far as possible, objectives should be quantifiable, although for most jobs there will be a mixture of hard objective measures and

competencies. Where competencies are used they should be carefully described in the form of demonstrable skills or behaviours that can be objectively assessed. At all costs, what must be avoided is any kind of trait approach which merely rates people on the basis of subjective descriptions such as 'appearance', 'personality', etc (see case study below).

■ Unfortunately, there are few short cuts when it comes to assessing performance. Careful consideration has to be given to each of the objectives and targets and account has to be taken of the circumstances in which they were achieved. There is rarely any easy formula that can be used for a particular measure.

■ In rating performance, the appraiser should take account of every aspect of the job, give an overall rating for the job as a whole and not be unduly influenced by extremes of performance in one part of it.

■ One of the greatest difficulties any manager experiences in appraising staff is being objective about the individual. There is a tendency, naturally, to want to give better ratings to people we like than to those we are less keen on. Similarly, judgement can be influenced by the 'halo effect' in which one impressive attribute can tend to make the appraiser rate the others more highly than they perhaps deserve. The converse could be described as the 'horns effect', in which poor performance in one area could colour judgements about other aspects.

■ In considering individual performance, emphasis should be placed on what are regarded as the priority objectives and the overall performance should be measured against the postholder's accountabilities.

■ Account should be taken of any internal factors affecting performance, such as changes to the organization, the availability of resources, the degree of challenge built into the accountabilities in the first place.

■ The appraiser should also take account of external circumstances, particularly in terms of market conditions, changes to the law or in government policies, and economic conditions. There are several examples of large divisionalized companies where some divisions are buoyant and managers are hitting their targets or exceeding them with ease, whereas in other divisions of the company, because of a difficult market, managers with similar targets struggle to get even close. In such circumstances account has to be taken of the prevalent market conditions, even at the risk of undermining what might be perceived as internal equity.

There are a number of different ways of describing the performance rating. Some organizations use a standard verbal description, others may assign an alphabetical or numerical rating, while yet others may describe performance as 'on target', 'above target', etc. Similarly the number of levels varies, with five being about the most common. The main danger with a five-point rating scale is that it tends to encourage raters to tick the middle box each time. However, it would be expected that most people in any organization, about 65–70 per cent, would fall into the middle category of

Case study — Trait based appraisal

One particular organization, a medium-sized company in the service sector, had a performance appraisal scheme which rated people on the basis of individual traits including, among others, 'intelligence'. It was not very surprising when one person raised a formal grievance about his rating under this heading, because his manager had used the phrase 'not very'.

You may wish to consider the following:

1. How does the trait based approach differ from a competency based approach?
2. What are the essential characteristics required of competencies to avoid them becoming just a wish-list?

satisfactory performance, assuming a normal distribution of talent and ability. Any severely skewed distribution, for example where over half the employees are classified as superior performers, would tend to suggest problems with how the performance standards are being applied and with the targets set. Some organizations claim that exceptional performance is the norm. If this is the case, then the targets set may be high compared with competitors but still only average within the organization, so a normal distribution of ratings would still be expected. There may, however, be some psychological merit in describing satisfactory performance as superior, provided all the other definitions are adapted accordingly. The most appropriate descriptions will depend on the culture of the organization.

Some examples of rating scales[3] are shown in Figure 5.3 and an example of an appraisal form is given at the end of the chapter.

Ensuring an effective performance appraisal

In undertaking the appraisal the appraiser should be aware of factors that can not only have an impact on performance, but also on the way the appraisal meeting goes. The kinds of factors that can affect attitudes include:

- the ages and experience of the appraiser and appraisee;
- their personalities and the extent to which these are compatible;
- the sex or ethnic origin of either party;
- how friendly or not they are;
- the appraisee's previous performance and the current trend — someone whose performance is improving is likely to be buoyant, whereas someone whose performance is declining may be defensive;
- the appraiser's fear of the appraisee's reaction — past studies have shown that one of the prime causes of performance appraisal failure is the reluctance on the part of managers to criticize performance where necessary.

There are a number of guidelines to be followed to ensure that any

---

Berisford International

1	Poor Performance
2	Acceptable
3	Average
4	Good
5	Outstanding

Barclays Bank:

Exceeded Contract (20% in this category in 1992)
Met Contract (70–75% in this category)
Fallen Short (5–7% in this category)

American Express (TRS):

G1	significantly exceeds customer requirements
G2	exceeds customer requirements
G3	meets all customer requirements
G4	meets most customer requirements
G5	does not meet customer requirements

Figure 5.3 *Some examples of rating scales*

appraisal interview goes well, by which we mean that both parties should emerge feeling that they had taken part in a useful and constructive discussion, with any areas of doubt clarified, and with the appraisee being left with the impression that the organization is concerned about his or her development. Some of the important rules to bear in mind are as follows:

- There should be careful planning of the meeting in advance. This means not only finding a quiet office with no interruptions, but also that the appraiser should have read all relevant documentation and gathered any necessary information. Similarly, the appraisee should have prepared for the meeting by reviewing his or her own performance and ideally should have been asked to rate it before the meeting. It is important to remember that the process is a two way one and that there should be no surprises for either party.
- The appraiser should ensure that the meeting is conducted in a supportive atmosphere and place emphasis on the counselling, coaching and developmental role that is part of the managerial responsibility.
- The emphasis should be, as far as possible, on the positive aspects of performance — not that the negative should be ignored, but the overall mood should be upbeat. It should be borne in mind, however, that most ambitious high-performers, while welcoming and needing the plaudits, are usually more interested in knowing where they have to improve.
- In discussing the less effective areas of performance, the opportunities for improvement should be stressed.
- The appraisee should be encouraged to talk, and the appraiser should discuss any problems, concerns or shortcomings and offer solutions where appropriate.

■ Actions should be agreed to resolve any identified problems and to develop the appraisee generally.

■ Following the meeting it should be ensured that whatever actions are agreed are taken, that track is kept of performance and that the positive aspects are continually reinforced.

■ Where performance ratings have a direct bearing on pay, this will tend to influence the appraisee's attitude towards the meeting. For this reason, it is better to keep pay-related discussions separate from appraisal interviews that are more concerned with the employee's development.

■ Finally, although it should not need to be stated, it is important to remember that the appraisal interview is confidential. It is inappropriate, for example, to draw comparisons between the appraisee's performance and that of other people or to discuss the ratings given to others.

The key to successful performance appraisal probably lies in ensuring that line managers have ownership of the process, that they are fully trained in it, and that there is general acceptance of the principle of appraisal by the employees concerned. The one thing that is certain is that individuals' performance will be appraised anyway. The issue is whether it should be done informally or formally and in an open and systematic way which can develop and reinforce a performance culture. However, once implemented, the process must be the only one in existence. There is at least one organization in which in addition to the formal scheme there was another, informal one through which managers could qualify any comments they might have made in face-to face discussion with the appraisee. These qualified comments could be made unofficially to senior members of management and would be placed on individuals' personal files. Obviously such an approach undermines the whole principle of performance management. Hopefully this example is an isolated one.

Rewarding Performance

Rewarding performance is the element of the performance management process which seeks to give employees some kind of return for achieving their targets. This is wider than just financial recompense and includes such things as praise, greater opportunities for training and development, and promotion. Very often one of the things most sought by an employee is the recognition that he or she is doing a good job and where, for example, this is expressed in terms of a bonus it is very often the recognition rather than the cash that really matters. It is only when money enters the equation that rewarding performance becomes very tricky, and the emphasis here is therefore on the financial aspects.

People very often consider performance management solely in terms of performance related pay (PRP). When there are business pressures to improve performance a common reaction of many managers is to want to pay for results, even though the organization may have no comprehensive system of performance management. However, it is never appropriate to introduce PRP unless there is already such a system in place. It is very difficult to get this aspect of the process right, and there are numerous examples of PRP schemes, which may be called 'merit pay', 'performance bonuses', 'incentive bonuses', etc, that have fallen into disrepute. For example, a recent in-depth study by the Institute of Manpower Studies in three organizations, a building society, a food retailer and a local authority, found that merit pay was more likely to demotivate than motivate employees. Similarly, a recent study of managers in British Telecom[4] found that some 63 per cent believed that PRP was applied unfairly. Both the London Borough of Lewisham and Sheffield City Council have abandoned their PRP schemes. At Lewisham it was reported that there had been no improvement in productivity, the performance element of salary was an insufficient incentive and many managers resented the scores they had been given. The Sheffield scheme has been described by the Council's Chief Personnel Officer as 'irrelevant at best and divisive at worst'.

Objectives of performance related pay[5]

Given that it is difficult to get it right, why do organizations seek to relate pay to performance and why is it apparently an increasing trend, particularly in the public sector and especially in those parts that have been recently privatized? The introduction of PRP can have a number of objectives:

- To motivate employees as they will see that their rewards are directly related to their efforts.
- To increase employees' focus on and commitment to corporate objectives.
- To help develop a performance culture or to reinforce the existing culture.
- To reward the contribution made by individuals to the organization's success (as distinct from the efforts put in).
- To help recruit and retain high-quality staff.
- To ensure that rewards are in line with organizational performance.
- For reasons of equity as it would be generally accepted that those who make the greatest contribution should receive the highest rewards.
- To assist in the achievement of organizational objectives by making these the basis on which any incentive payments are made.
- To encourage a focus on individual or team performance, depending on which is the more appropriate for the organization's needs.

Arguments for and against PRP[6]

Arguments for and against PRP are summarized in Table 5.1.

Table 5.1 *Arguments for and against PRP*

For	Against
It seems only fair that those who make the greatest contribution to the organization should receive the highest rewards, rather than rewards being based solely on long service.	It is very difficult to measure performance accurately and this is especially true of managerial, professional and administrative jobs. Any assessment of performance is bound to be subjective, which in turn can lead to unfair ratings and reward allocation.
While many people may not be motivated by money, most would like recognition and the ability to pay a performance bonus is a means of indicating to the individual that his or her contribution is valued.	Money does not motivate — there is significant research and empirical evidence to suggest that a large number of people are not motivated by cash rewards and that those who are most likely to receive the rewards will be the highest motivated in any case.
The process of identifying performance objectives and incentivizing them should help provide a focus on the issues of importance to the organization.	It could tend to make people focus more on short-term outputs and on those that will bring rewards, at a possible cost in terms of quality and longer-term development.
The continuing growth in PRP schemes means that there is an expectation on the part of postholders that superior performance will be rewarded by some kind of incentive — not to give such a reward could itself be demotivating.	PRP can sometimes be used as a means of compensating for lower base pay which can result in the pay policy being distorted and the incentive element being lost.
Carefully designed schemes can help communicate clear messages about organizational performance.	Too much emphasis on individual performance could undermine teamwork.
	It can be divisive, especially if people feel that rewards are being allocated unfairly.
	There is little evidence to suggest that it actually improves performance.
	It can undermine the performance appraisal process as the appraisee may feel that the outcome will affect pay.
	Such schemes can increase the overall pay bill unless there are very tight controls.

Conditions for the successful introduction of PRP

For PRP to be introduced successfully, the following factors must be obtained:

■ The scheme must be appropriate to the organization's culture. There is no such thing as an off-the-shelf scheme, and in some cases it may not be appropriate to have any scheme at all.

- The scheme must be closely linked to a comprehensive performance management process. Without such a process, PRP cannot be expected to work effectively.
- The performance management process must include a robust mechanism for setting objectives and targets that meet the criteria set out earlier in this chapter, and for reviewing and assessing performance against these.
- There has to be top management commitment to the process, so that it is owned by line managers and not merely seen as a personnel system.
- While the measures on which performance is judged should as far as possible be quantifiable and objective, some more objective ones will inevitably need to be included.
- One of the key considerations is to ensure that the managers operating the scheme are thoroughly trained in its principles.
- The scheme should be sufficiently flexible to be able to take account of changes in business circumstances or in the circumstances of individuals.
- The link between the financial rewards and performance must be a clear one and should be effectively communicated to employees.
- There is a need to ensure that performance measures are not just quantitative but are also qualitative in nature including, for example, such measures as teamwork and innovation.
- The rewards should be seen to be appropriate in terms of the effort put in and the results produced. If they are regarded as derisory the scheme will soon fall into disrepute.
- In goal setting, account should be taken of the need to achieve long-term objectives as well as short-term ones, and any PRP scheme should be designed to reward both.
- The scheme should concentrate rewards in those areas of the business that are deemed to be of prime importance. In other words, if it is the intention of the organization to try to improve return on capital employed, then this should be one of the factors that is incentivized.
- The percentage of base salary or the size of sums paid out should be related to the nature of the organization and the type of work undertaken. For example, in a sharp-end sales job in a competitive market it could well be that 100 per cent of salary is performance related. However, this would be entirely inappropriate for an office based clerical or professional job.
- Jobs must be clearly defined and accountabilities spelt out, if individuals are to achieve the required results.
- Finally, there should be total clarity about why the process is being introduced and what it is to achieve. Without this clarity it is better not to proceed.

INTRODUCING PERFORMANCE MANAGEMENT

Returning to performance management as a whole, to ensure its successful introduction the following principles should be adhered to:

1. It should link clearly with and support the organization's mission and core values and relate closely to its corporate strategy.

2. It must be in line with and appropriate to the organization's culture.

3. The process must have the commitment of top management and be owned by the line managers. (*Mixtin*)

4. There should, as far as possible, be joint discussions and employee involvement in the development of the scheme supported by comprehensive communication about it and thorough training of everyone involved.

5. The scheme should be supported by a comprehensive system of objective and target setting and clear job descriptions stating accountabilities.

6. The scheme should be kept under constant review and changes made as necessary.

7. The individual development aspects of performance management should be kept separate from reward considerations.

8. No link should be made with pay until the scheme has been running effectively for some time and is generally accepted throughout the organization.

Many of these principles underlie the scheme operated by the London Borough of Bexley described in the following case study.

Case Study — London Borough of Bexley

Objectives

The London Borough of Bexley has a comprehensive Staff Appraisal and Performance Related Pay Scheme which has the following objectives:

- To ensure that staff know what they are required to do and how performance will be assessed.
- To help staff develop the skills necessary to ensure success and prepare for promotion.
- To provide a mechanism for staff to discuss job performance with their managers and benefit from feedback.
- To ensure that fair and objective assessment of performance is made for the purpose of salary progression.
- To provide each employee with a record of service and achievement in Bexley.

The aim is to improve the Council's overall performance by helping individual members of staff improve their own performance.

Planning Performance

Staff performance plans are based on three elements:

1. *Accountability statements*, usually between six and eight in number, which define the key outcomes for posts.
2. *Effectiveness indicators*, which are the measures against which each accountability is assessed.
3. *Annual supplements*, which are specific tasks or projects undertaken in addition to the postholder's accountabilities.

In addition, six main areas are defined for the assignment of accountabilities. These are:

1. *Strategy* — assisting in the formulation of the Council's objectives.
2. *Direction* — producing and communicating operational plans.
3. *Implementation* — providing services within the set time and cost constraints and to the required standards.
4. *Organizational control and development* — maintaining and developing the Council's structure and processes.
5. *Staff management and development* — recruitment, management and development of staff to achieve existing objectives and meet future challenges.
6. *Personal effectiveness* — maintain and develop full range of relevant knowledge and skills.

It is envisaged that the above headings should cover the full range of accountabilities for most jobs although, exceptionally, there may be other specific accountabilities.

Reviewing Performance

There are three formal appraisal meetings a year:

■ A review of accountabilities and agreement of specific tasks and projects for the year.
■ An intermediate (six monthly) assessment to review progress and performance.
■ An end of year assessment to rate the employee's performance in each accountability area and award of a final performance category based on the full year. The ratings are:
  1. Superior all round performance — notable objectives achieved which will bring lasting benefits.
  2. Performance generally exceeds job requirements — some significant achievements.
  3. Performance generally satisfies job requirements.
  4. Satisfactory performance in most aspects of the job with some improvement required.
  5. Significant improvement required to satisfy job requirements.

The final performance category is awarded by the appraiser's manager (the grandparent). Categories 1 and 2 can only be awarded by a Chief Officer. The appraisee has a right of appeal to the grandparent's manager.

Rewarding Performance

While the appraisal process is seen as providing an opportunity to focus on training and development needs, the performance category awarded will also have a direct impact on the appraisee's salary progression. This is determined by the use of a salary progression matrix which takes account of the employee's current position in the pay range.

If there is one single message that we would like any reader to take away from this chapter it is that performance management is a process and not a one-off event. It is really a way of managing and of ensuring that the organization achieves its objectives. Managers do not have a choice about whether or not they do it. The key role of the manager is to ensure that the people of the organization perform as effectively as possible to help achieve the objectives identified. This means managing their performance and developing what we would describe as a performance culture.

Effective performance management is central to the success of the organization as people are probably the greatest variable and are likely to be the crucial difference between success or failure. It also has implications for all the other systems of the organization including recruitment, pay and benefits, training and development and employee relations. It is too important not to get it right.

References

1 Spencer, L M, McClelland, D C and Spencer, S M (1992) *Competency Assessment Methods — History and State of the Art*, Hay/McBer Boston, MA.

2 Sheard, A (1992) 'Learning to improve performance', *Personnel Management*, November.

3 *Management Bonus Schemes*, Research File 28, Incomes Data Services Ltd, November 1993.

4 *More stressing performance: a report on performance pay, workloads and stress in BT*, Society of Telecom Executives, STE Research, London.

5 Armstrong, M and Murlis, H (1991) *Reward Management: A Handbook of Remuneration Strategy and Practice*, Kogan Page, London.

6 *Performance-Related Pay*, Personnel Management Factsheet No 30, June 1990.

Training and Development

This chapter is concerned with the process of training and development in the organization. It is important to remember, however, that the training and development of employees does not happen in isolation and is linked in some way with all the aspects of human resource management. The recruitment process, for example, will need to take into account the skills required by a person to be able to undertake effectively the duties of the post in question and those making the selection will be looking for evidence of these skills. Similarly, effective performance will be dependent on postholders not only being clear about their objectives but also being fully trained to achieve them. The safety of employees, especially in an industrial environment, is crucially dependent on their being trained in safe methods of working which in turn will reduce accidents and time off and improve productivity. The links between training and development and other processes of human resource management are summarized in Figure 6.1.

This whole area is covered in depth in the *Human Resource Development* title in this series[1] and readers are recommended to turn to that for further information.

Where training ends and development begins is a very blurred line and for the purposes of this chapter the two have been treated as largely indistinguishable. Where there is a difference it is mainly in terms of emphasis.

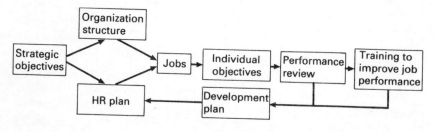

Figure 6.1 *The training and development process*

DEFINITIONS

Training

Training is the process by which people are taught skills and given the necessary knowledge or attitude to enable them to carry out their responsibilities to the required standard. It is different from education which imparts general knowledge of a particular subject, as it is focused on the specific requirements of a job. Usually the aims are to improve the performance of current tasks, to instruct in the carrying out of tasks with which the postholder is not familiar, or to prepare the individual for changes that are likely to arise.

A comprehensive definition of training formulated by the Manpower Services Commission[2] is as follows:

> a planned process to modify attitude, knowledge or skill behaviour through learning experience to achieve effective performance in an activity or range of activities. Its purpose, in the work situation, is to develop the abilities of the individual and to satisfy the current and future manpower needs of the organization.

It is difficult to overestimate the importance of effective training. Many systems (particularly computer systems) which might otherwise have operated effectively fail because their users are inadequately trained. Also, as indicated above, effective training is a crucial element of effective performance.

Development

Whereas training is concerned with equipping staff to carry out their responsibilities to the required standard in the present job, development is concerned with giving individuals the necessary knowledge, skills and experience to enable them to undertake greater and more demanding roles and responsibilities. In current thinking there is particular emphasis on teaching people how to develop themselves, a theme which should underpin the whole approach to performance management, considered in detail in Chapter 5. The Institute of Personnel and Development Code of Professional Conduct describes the development of others as 'the fullest possible development of the capabilities of individual employees to meet present and future requirements of the organisation and ... to develop themselves.'

The Manpower Services Commission definition[3] is:

> The growth or realisation of a person's ability, through conscious or unconscious learning. Development programmes usually include elements of planned study and experience, and are frequently supported by a coaching or counselling facility.

Development is often categorized in terms of management development, organization development (commonly referred to as OD) and staff development. In particular, there has always been a strong emphasis on management development. This is perhaps hardly surprising since it is crucial that the organization's managers are equipped to adapt to change and have all the necessary attributes to enable them to make decisions critical to the organization's success. Because the organization may not always be able to, or wish to, recruit suitable managers it is clearly necessary for it to be able to grow its own. There is in any case an expectation, particularly on the part of talented and ambitious high-flyers, that such development opportunities will be provided for them. Without it they may not remain for very long.

Whereas management development concentrates on the individual manager, organization development is about the development of the whole organization, or at least certain parts of it. While management and staff development are part of this process OD is more concerned about total organizational effectiveness, or organizational health and the ability of the organization to adapt to change. It comprises a whole range of strategies, techniques and approaches, usually called interventions, aimed at individuals, groups, teams and, ultimately, the whole organization. The emphasis is on cultural change.

THE PURPOSE OF TRAINING

The main reason for undertaking training is for the organization to ensure that it achieves the best possible return from its investment in its most important (and frequently most expensive) resource: its employees. To this effect, the main aim of any training will be to achieve some kind of change in knowledge, skills, experience, behaviour or attitude which enhances the effectiveness of the employee. Specifically, training will be used to:

- develop individual skills and abilities to improve job performance;
- familiarize employees with new systems, procedures and methods of working;
- help employees and new starters to become familiar with the requirements of a particular job and of the organization.

It is generally accepted that the most difficult aspect of training is changing attitudes and behaviour, compared to which improvements in knowledge and skills are relatively straightforward to attain and measure.

INTRODUCING A TRAINING STRATEGY

Training, like any of the organization's other activities should be planned and should relate to the organization's corporate strategy. The organization's mission and goals will determine its corporate objectives. These objectives should in turn determine the numbers, levels and types of staff required to attain them. For individual jobs there should be job descriptions outlining a post's accountabilities or key result areas and these will, in turn, suggest the education, knowledge, skill and possibly competence requirements of a particular post. These requirements will form the personnel specification for the post. Having determined the requirements of the job, the next stage is to analyse any shortfalls in the individual which might prevent him or her from carrying out the responsibilities effectively, ie the training gap. This process is summarized in Figure 6.2.

Armstrong[4] states that training should not be regarded simply as an act of faith but that it 'must be supported by a positive and realistic philosophy of how training contributes to organisational success'. Certainly the organization should have a clear view of how it regards training, otherwise there is the danger of a *laissez-faire* attitude in which training, if it happens at all, will be unplanned and haphazard. This kind of approach is clearly wasteful of time and resources. On the other hand, the organization could decide that the most economic approach is to buy in people with the necessary knowledge, skills and experience rather than invest money itself in training.

Whatever approach is decided on, it should be part of a conscious and rational decision rather than something that happens by default. As indicated by the definition above, all training should be part of a systematic and planned programme.

The introduction of any training policy will need to incorporate the following stages:

1.   An analysis of training needs.
2.   A planned programme of training to meet those needs.
3.   Implementation of the training programme.
4.   An evaluation of the effectiveness of the training provided.

These are considered in turn below.

Analysis of training needs

It is essential that any training provided is based on a systematic analysis of its contribution to the effectiveness of the organization. This involves

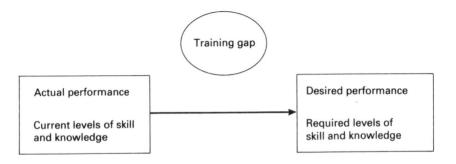

Figure 6.2 *The training gap*

defining training needs and assessing to what extent barriers to the achievement of organizational objectives may be removed by training.

A training need exists when a particular weakness may be overcome by the application of suitable training. These needs should be assessed at three levels:

1. At organizational level.
2. At group or occupational level.
3. At the individual level.

The starting point for analysing needs at the organizational level should be the corporate strategy. Once the organization's key objectives have been determined and the critical success factors identified, it should be possible to identify areas of actual or potential weakness that may be corrected by training. This should all be apparent from the human resource plan which will identify the numbers, types and levels of employee required to meet existing and future needs.

The organization has to take account of a range of factors that are likely to affect its training requirements. These include the following:

- *Staff turnover* — the greater the number of new recruits, the greater will be the need for training in job skills and for induction training.
- *Changes in technology* — new systems and processes will require staff to be fully trained in their application; many new computer systems fail not for technical reasons but because staff have not been trained how to use them.
- *Changes in jobs* — jobs invariably change over time, especially as the organization itself changes, and employees need to be trained to adapt.
- *Changes in legislation* — changes in the law or in government regulations will frequently mean that new systems and approaches are required, and this is particularly true of the impact of the EU on employment law.
- *Economic developments* — in a recession companies are particularly concerned about reducing costs and maximizing productivity, which implies having better trained staff who have a range of skills so that they can be used flexibly by the organization.
- *New patterns of work* — increased homeworking, for example, gives the organization and its employees more flexibility, but requires a different approach from office based employment and might entail a need to acquire new skills.
- *Market pressures* — the need to remain competitive means that the organization has to ensure that employees are aware of latest developments and have the skills to innovate.
- *Social policies* — privatization, for example, means that public sector employees have to acquire new commercial skills.
- *Employee aspirations* — the need to attract and retain staff of a suitable calibre means that employers have to offer training and development opportunities; failure to do so can have an adverse effect on an organization's image.

- *Performance variations* — where there are significant variations in performance between one part of the organization and another, this can reveal a need for training (although many other factors can be operating).
- *Equality of opportunity* — the organization may have to run training programmes to ensure that particular groups such as the disabled, members of ethnic minorities or women are not disadvantaged, especially where promotion prospects are concerned.

At group or occupational level needs can best be determined by job analysis and by analysing performance and productivity. This will identify the accountabilities and tasks of various jobs and, for the purposes of performance management and training, should also set out performance criteria and standards, and identify the levels of knowledge, skills and experience required to meet those standards.

Obviously such comparisons can also be made at the organizational level as part of a benchmarking exercise.

At the individual level needs can best be assessed through a comprehensive performance management process, as described in Chapter 5. A key part of any performance appraisal should be a review of areas in which existing performance can be improved by training and where development may be necessary to equip the postholder to undertake a more demanding role.

There are a number of other ways of identifying training needs, such as undertaking detailed task analyses, through a problem centred approach (such as all staff requiring training in a new piece of legislation), interpersonal skills analysis, and the FDI approach in which tasks are reviewed in terms of their Frequency, Difficulty and Importance. Training needs can also be identified by interviewing postholders, by asking them to complete questionnaires and by observation.

In management development and professional staff development there is an increasing tendency to use a competency based approach in which the key competencies for superior, or at least fully effective, performance are identified and the staff concerned then trained in these competencies. This kind of approach seeks to change behaviour and attitudes rather than teach skills. Methods of identifying and measuring competencies are set out in Figure 6.3.

Activity — Performance indicators as determinants of training need

List those measures and performance indicators that might indicate a need for training, eg accident rates.

Planning training

In planning training programmes there are a number of factors to be taken into account. These include:

Competencies	Measurement Techniques			
	Personality Questionnaire	Tests	Interview	Exercises
Understanding what needs to be done Reasoning ability Knowledge Skills		• • •	•	• •
Influencing and gaining support Presentation Interpersonal Persuading	• •		• •	• • •
Producing the results Directing Motivating Productivity	• • •		• • •	• • •
Achieving against the odds Enterprise Confidence Achievement Resilience	• • • •	• • •	• • •	• • • •

Figure 6.3 *Identifying and measuring competencies*
Source: MSL Human Resource Consultants

- the objectives of the training;
- the content of the training;
- the recipients of the training;
- the likely costs involved;
- the costs of not training;
- the likely benefits and how they can be evaluated;
- the various training methods available and their appropriateness;
- the location and timing of any training programme;
- who will provide the training.

Setting objectives

Before formulating any training programme it is necessary to be clear about the required outcomes, since if your destination is unknown how will you know when you have arrived or what route to take? This certainly applies to any training course which should always begin by stating its objectives. Very often these will be stated in terms of what the individual will be expected to be able to do when he or she returns to the workplace.

As with any kind of objective, objectives for training should be as specific as possible, otherwise it will be difficult to assess whether they have been achieved. Clear objectives are also important to help ensure that the right people are given the right programmes.

Programme content

The content of any training programme will be determined by what the programme is seeking to achieve and by the prospective trainees. It should be formulated to meet the needs identified by an analysis of training needs as described above.

The trainees

It is clearly very important to take account of the types of job and the kinds of postholder who are to be trained. This will determine the level at which the training should be pitched and the way in which the training programme is constructed. If the training is for blue-collar employees who are used to carrying out practical tasks and are not accustomed to sitting in lecture rooms, the programme will need to have a high practical content with a minimum of 'chalk and talk'. Even for office based personnel there should be as much practical content as possible, and lectures should be kept brief.

The ages, knowledge and experience of the trainees are also of crucial importance. It is very difficult to run an effective training programme where the trainees all have different levels of understanding. This is where good training records, careful selection of trainees and clear descriptions of objectives and content are so important.

Likely costs

There are a number of costs associated with any training programme, although these will vary greatly with the type of training provided. The costs are likely to include:

- the hire of suitable accommodation for any training course (or the costs of running a training centre, if the organization is large);
- the hire of suitable lecturers or facilitators and salaries of staff carrying out these and other organizing roles;
- travelling and subsistence expenses;
- salaries and benefits of trainees;
- lost production because of trainees' absence from the workplace and costs of providing cover;
- provision of suitable course materials;
- staff time spent in arranging training programme;
- possible increased costs of recruitment as trained staff become more in demand by other employers;
- in some circumstances, increased pay costs as employees reach certain

pre-determined standards (in the UK water industry, for example, craftsmen reaching certain skill levels, which are clearly set out, will usually be placed in a higher grade).

Costs of not training

Given the array of costs set out above, perhaps it is not surprising that when finances are tight the training budget is one of the first things to be cut. However, this is a short-sighted approach as there are a number of costs associated with *not* training. These include:

■ the need for additional recruitment to buy in skills not available within the organization and to replace staff who leave because of a lack of training opportunities;
■ reduced productivity arising from less efficient working methods or less developed skills;
■ the longer time taken for individuals to become fully proficient;
■ a reduced ability to adapt to changing conditions or to innovate;
■ an increased likelihood of accidents;
■ a less motivated workforce with consequent lower productivity;
■ less awareness of, and commitment to, organizational objectives.

The fact is that whether or not there is an effective training policy and programme, employees will still learn a particular way of carrying out their responsibilities. The problem is that the methods learnt may not be the most efficient or effective and may not be consistent with the organization's mission and objectives.

Benefits of training and their evaluation

In many cases the benefits may not be very obvious or easy to measure. Indeed management development, for example, has been described as an 'act of faith' because it is very difficult to demonstrate measurable improvements. This problem of evaluating training is considered in more detail later in this chapter.

When it comes to deciding where the training priorities should lie, one of the factors will be the likely benefits. The main focus should be on those areas considered critical to the success of the business, and where there is considered to be a shortfall between the required levels of knowledge and skills and those actually existing. This will depend on the training needs identified through the needs analysis described earlier.

Other things being equal, it is probably wise to concentrate on those areas of training where there is a demonstrable return to the organization.

Available training methods

There are a variety of training methods, the most appropriate depending mainly on the type of training to be provided and the trainees. Often there is a tendency to think of training as going on courses, to the neglect of the many other approaches available. In general these various approaches may be divided into on-the-job and off-the-job, although both contexts may be used in some circumstances.

The various training methods and techniques are outlined later in this chapter.

Location

The initial question in planning the location of any training is whether it should be held within the organization or off-site. A second question is, assuming that it is to be held within the organization, should it be on-the-job or off-the-job?

There is a wealth of external training available and the main advantage is that it is generally possible to find a course that meets the organization's requirements, particularly where general management, professional, administrative and supervisory skills are concerned, and that will be run by professionals with a known reputation. Using such sources is likely to be cheaper and more convenient than an organization taking the time, effort and cost to develop its own training courses (except where substantial numbers are involved). Where there is a continuing need over a long period and the organization has unique requirements that cannot easily be met by external courses, there may be justification for developing in-house programmes.

The main disadvantage of external training is what has been described as the 're-entry problem'. Techniques and approaches learnt on courses may not readily transfer to certain organization cultures. Many people will have heard variants of the phrase, 'That's all very well in theory but it won't work here.' On the other hand, external courses do enable participants to mix with other people from all kinds of organizations so ideas can be exchanged.

Where training is to be held internally the main issue to consider is whether it is to be as part of the job or as a separate learning experience. Where it is carried out as part of the job through instruction by managers or colleagues, the effectiveness of the training will naturally depend on the quality of the instruction. Generally this approach is more suited to relatively straightforward jobs and as a supplement to other training methods.

Training off-the-job but within the organization can be very effective as it takes individuals away from the work environment and enables them to concentrate on learning without distractions. Furthermore the tutors are likely to be highly experienced members of the organization who can be relied on to teach sound working methods. Again, however, there can be a re-entry problem, although it is likely to be less pronounced than with external courses.

Who should provide training?

Training may be provided by a number of different people. These can be in-house trainers and instructors, external lecturers, and the trainees' managers, supervisors and colleagues. Where the organization has a large number of specialist roles, such as in British Gas, employing in-house trainers is probably the most cost-effective approach. The use of external lecturers is more appropriate for subjects of general applicability and especially for management training, as the trainees will benefit from an external perspective. Against this, in-house trainers will have a better understanding of the organization's culture and will know what is acceptable and what is not. Finally, the use of in-house mentors is particularly valuable, and should be part of the manager's coaching role.

ON-THE-JOB TRAINING

The main on-the-job techniques are:

- demonstration;
- coaching;
- do-it-yourself training;
- job rotation and planned experience;
- technology based training (TBT).

Demonstration

Demonstration, or 'sitting next to Nellie' as it is sometimes called, is probably the most common form of training. It involves the trainee being shown how to perform a task or a series of tasks by an experienced employee and then being left to get on with it. The main problem with this form of training is that if the operator demonstrating the tasks has acquired bad habits or has failed to understand certain parts of the job, these bad habits and misunderstandings are likely to be passed on to the trainee. Similarly any negative attitudes about the organization or unauthorized short-cuts in working methods are also likely to be acquired. It is however, probably the simplest, quickest and most cost-effective way of enabling the trainee to learn the job, provided it is properly controlled.

Coaching

Coaching differs from demonstration in being more of a way of managing staff than a direct means of passing on detailed instructions. The trainee is given general support and guidance, with the emphasis more on helping the individual teach himself or herself and on ensuring that he or she acquires the necessary knowledge, skills and experience. It is particularly appropriate for managerial and professional jobs and where it is part of the development of a performance culture, and is described in more detail in Chapter 5 on performance management.

Do-It-Yourself training

Do-it-yourself training is based on the discovery method of learning, which assumes that the most effective way of learning is when the trainee has to find out for himself or herself. The approach entails being very clear in the first place about what the trainee needs to know to carry out his or her responsibilities effectively, establishing where the information may be obtained, and then giving the trainee an outline of the information required and perhaps setting projects based on this. It is part of a planned programme with regular reports back to someone, such as the employee's line manager, who is responsible for monitoring progress and providing guidance.

Job rotation and planned experience

Job rotation consists of moving employees into other jobs for a period to enable them to acquire new and wider skills. It is particularly appropriate in modern organizations where lean staff structures mean that there is a greater need for employees to be very flexible and to have a range of skills. It can also be very useful in promoting greater understanding between different parts of the organization. There is no better way to appreciate the problems and frustrations of someone's job than by doing it yourself.

Any job rotation should be part of a planned programme and can sometimes be used not just for training and development purposes, but also as a means of rewarding staff for whom there are no immediate promotion opportunities. Needless to say, it is particularly appropriate for management development.

As an alternative to rotating jobs, which does bring with it problems of managing differences in salaries and locations and of continuity in the workplace, employees can be appointed to project teams where they can have the opportunity to work with staff from other disciplines and to consider problems outside their immediate experience.

Where planned experience tends to fall down is when trainees are unceremoniously dumped in a department without warning and the manager has to find something to occupy their time. This becomes an unpleasant experience for both parties, with the trainees feeling unwelcome and usually being given some undesirable or meaningless task and with the manager resenting being dragged away from his or her main work just to find some form of occupational therapy. Any such programme must be carefully planned, with agreed objectives, monitoring of progress and full consultation with any managers involved.

One radical approach developed by Rolls-Royce[5] and designed to strengthen commercial skills and provide more flexibility, but which avoids the above pitfall, was the setting up of a real company, Flexible Local Engineering Enterprise Training (or FLEET), run by students and providing a range of services to other parts of the group on a non-profit basis. The students have real responsibilities and derive the additional benefit of working in multidisciplinary teams.

Technology based training

Technology based training refers to any desk based technique which enables the individual to work through a training programme using interactive computer programs, videos or compact discs. Such applications are likely to become more powerful as computer based multimedia systems develop and their full training potential is realized.

OFF-THE-JOB TRAINING

Some of the main off-the-job training techniques are:

- lectures;
- case studies;
- role playing;
- discussion groups;
- development centres;
- group dynamics;
- action learning;
- projects;
- business games;
- outdoor training.

Lectures

Everyone is familiar with lectures, one of the most common ways of imparting knowledge, particularly for educational purposes. Everyone also probably recalls the main drawback to them, ie being able to sustain students' attention for their duration. Memories of boring hours spent trying to keep awake while uninspired lecturers drone on about subjects that are of no interest to us are part of everyone's experience. For this reason there may often be an in-built resistance to this specific form of training.

The main problem with lectures is probably that they are one way, with little interaction between lecturer and students. For this reason it is crucial that the lecturer tries to make the subject as interesting as possible and indeed encourages student participation. Even so, it is generally agreed that only about 20 per cent of what is said will be retained. This retention rate can be improved if the learning is reinforced by the students putting the lessons into practice soon afterwards. It is also generally accepted that the average attention span is relatively short, perhaps only up to 20 minutes or so; therefore lectures should be kept as short as possible or be interspersed with breaks.

Case studies

Case studies are short histories or descriptions, often based on real events, which are used to help in the diagnosis and solution of problems. They can be used to teach trainees the appropriate questions to ask and the factors that need to be taken into account. In one variant of the case study approach students are only given some of the information required to make a decision and it is up to them to realize that more is needed and to ask for this from the tutor. In another, called the incident method, the study consists only of a short statement describing an incident which has taken place and to which the trainee has to react. To make case studies authentic requires careful planning and probably the main drawback is that they may not be perceived as reflecting reality. Decisions made in a classroom take little account of environment.

Role playing

In role playing trainees consider problems in much the same way as in case studies, except that a number of people play different roles. Individuals are usually given a brief on the kind of role they are to play. The value of this kind of exercise is that it can give an insight into a different point of view. In industrial relations training, for example, a manager might play the part of a shop steward and vice versa. Although it does help in the perception of the other's role, there is often a tendency for this approach to bring out the frustrated thespian in many people and for them to enter into the whole affair with too much gusto. On the other hand, there are others who feel inhibited and embarrassed by the whole process. To be of value role playing must be treated seriously, although sometimes people take it too seriously and end up upsetting someone else.

Discussion groups

Active group discussions are valuable for bringing out a variety of views on any particular topic, and their participative nature usually ensures that they retain the interest of the trainees. They can take many different forms including, for example, a so-called 'goldfish bowl' exercise in which one group holds a discussion while another group observes their interactions. In general such groups enable those present to learn from the experience of others and to practise and improve their own skills of self-expression. There is, however, always the danger that such groups may be dominated by the articulate few.

Development centres[6]

A development centre is a variant of the assessment centre in which a whole battery of tests, such as psychometric assessment, group discussions, in-tray exercises, etc are used on a group of people in a training centre to assess their skills, competencies or knowledge, and therefore their suitability for certain roles. The development centre takes the assessment centre a stage further and attempts to empower people to develop their potential through behaviourally anchored development plans. For example, Yorkshire Water uses development centres with a long-term aim of personal development and career management for senior managers, while the National Health Service, with consultancy support, has used them to help women equip themselves to undertake senior managerial responsibilities, breaking through the 'glass ceiling'.

Group dynamics

Group dynamics refers to a whole range of techniques designed to improve group effectiveness and based on behavioural science research. Probably the best known of these techniques is the T-group, the T standing for training. Other techniques include Coverdale training, the use of the Blake and Mouton managerial grid, Reddin's 3D organizational effectiveness, the Hersey and Blanchard situational leadership model, and the Belbin team roles model.

Action learning

Action learning is an approach developed by Revans[7] which is based on the principle that people learn best by doing. His approach, which is aimed primarily at managers, exposes people to real problems about which they are required to take action (not just to make recommendations or undertake analysis). They may be required to tackle problems similar to those they are familiar with but in a different environment, or unfamiliar problems in a familiar environment. This is illustrated by the matrix shown in Figure 6.4. The most demanding learning environment, and the one that is ultimately likely to be the most rewarding, is one in which the trainee deals with new problems in an unfamiliar environment.

Projects

Designing projects to develop a person's knowledge and research skills is

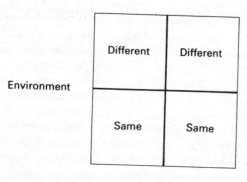

Problems

Figure 6.4 *An action learning matrix*

something that can be done either within or outside the work environment. Similarly the project can be for an individual or a team. With a team approach there is the added benefit of team building or the development of cooperative skills. Ideally, the project should be something of practical value to the organization otherwise trainees may not feel committed to it, and because it thereby becomes a more productive use of time.

Business games

Business games or exercises can take many different forms, but generally consist of teams of players competing against each other in what might be a simulation of a real-life situation or something rather more abstract. In one particular game, of which there are a number of variants, teams are encouraged to build up scores by forming alliances with each other and by negotiating deals. Very often the results can be manipulated by the tutors to give what looks like an unfair advantage to one team or another. This kind of game can be a powerful demonstration of how well certain negotiating stances work and also of how easily group identities can be formed (and undermined) by circumstances. The main problem with these kinds of game is that they are often regarded as no more than a game, even though emotions can sometimes run high during them.

Outdoor development

There has been a growth in the use of outdoor development training in recent years, based on the premise that outward-bound type training that places people in challenging situations will help to develop leadership and team skills. After all, a similar approach is used in the training of officers in the armed forces. There has been some scepticism about whether this actually works and whether the kinds of situation encountered in this type of training can really help in the business environment. Certainly it does seem to be a developmental experience for some people, however on the whole the case is probably not proven.

NATIONAL VOCATIONAL QUALIFICATIONS (NVQS)

National vocational qualifications or NVQs are an attempt in the UK to establish a national framework of qualifications based on common national standards. The concept is a sound one as it would mean that instead of numerous different vocational qualifications of varying standards, with a consequent difficulty of comparing one with another, there would be one standard for all. NVQs also emphasize practical ability or competence in the tasks the individual has to carry out to agreed standards, rather than academic ability. There are five levels of NVQ and competence is assessed in the workplace under normal working conditions.

NVQs have received something of a mixed reaction, and some organizations, British Home Stores for example, have even abandoned them after a period. This seems to be partly because of the difficulty of defining the competency levels and also because of the tendency for jargon to be overused. According to one report almost half a group of trainers in local government found the standards difficult to comprehend. However, the training coordinator at Booker Cash and Carry is quoted by *Personnel Management* as saying that 'they encourage teamwork and lead to greater job satisfaction and lower turnover'.

IMPLEMENTING TRAINING PROGRAMMES

Once training has been thoroughly planned the next stage is to implement it. At this point:

1. The organizer should be entirely clear about the objectives of the training.
2. The target group should have been identified.
3. The training needs should have been identified.
4. The form of training should have been decided on.
5. The costs and potential benefits should have been calculated.

The exact form of the training will depend on the people to be trained and the objectives of the training. If the training is for induction purposes, for example, it would be expected that it would consist almost entirely of an in-house programme involving a number of meetings and discussions with other staff. A management development programme, on the other hand, would be more likely to comprise periods of planned experience supplemented by attendance at external courses of training or education, and possibly also the use of a development centre.

Case Study — Management development at Pilkington[6]

The Pilkington Group is well aware of the problem of translating classroom learning into the work environment and has sought to overcome this by combining an assessment centre with their development programme. The programme:

- identifies development priorities through the systematic comparison of job requirements and personal skills;
- sets clear, work-related targets;
- asks participants to design cost-effective learning methods that make a direct and significant contribution to their jobs;
- uses previous participants as coaches and train them in development planning;
- provides development planning rules and monitors them;
- arranges for each participant with his or her coach to agree a development plan with his or her manager;
- arranges for the personnel director to meet the participants before and after the course to discuss reports and plans;
- monitors results by questionnaire and feedback six months after the programme.

The main concern at the implementation stage is that the administrative arrangements work well. While this can often be the most aggravating, time consuming, frustrating and least interesting part of the whole process, it is essential that things run smoothly otherwise even the best designed programme is likely to lose credibility.

MANAGEMENT DEVELOPMENT

Although training and development have been treated here as virtually indistinguishable, there are certain key considerations when designing management development programmes that merit special mention. These are:

- As far as possible, learning should be based on the consideration of real problems in real environments.
- Development should be of groups as well as individuals.
- Development must be linked to effective selection as there is little point in trying to make a silk purse out of a sow's ear.
- Learning techniques should be appropriate to the aims of the programme.
- There must be organizational commitment to development.
- Those responsible for the development of managers should themselves be adequately trained.
- Development programmes should be integrated with the organization's corporate strategy.
- Development should take account of individual needs and perceptions.
- The programme should take account of the organization's culture.
- There should be mechanisms for assessing the effectiveness of any development programme.

Of course, many of these principles are equally applicable to other kinds of development. They are all based on experience of what can go wrong in the design of management development programmes.

When designing management development programmes it is important to bear in mind the growth in demand as companies become more international for what are often described as Euro-managers, capable of operating in a number of different countries. In one sector, water for example, there has been an increasing involvement of French companies such as SAUR and the utilities giant Compagnie Générale des Eaux in UK water operations.

This trend is likely to lead to more international training and development programmes such as that set up by the German chemical multinational Hoechst. This is a two-year programme incorporating work experience and designed to build a more international outlook among managers. Development in general has a high profile in this company which is training up to 6000 apprentices at any one time.

There is a contrast in the way in which different countries develop their

LIVERPOOL JOHN MOORES UNIVERSITY
LEARNING SERVICES

managers. In the UK and the United States, for example, there is a tendency for managers to be generalists with any kind of academic background being viewed as suitable. The position is similar in France, particularly for graduates of the *grandes écoles*. In Germany there is more functional specialization and generalist management roles are higher up the organization structure. However, with the need for more flexible and responsive structures there is now a tendency in companies such as Siemens to move general management lower down the structure — greater empowerment, if you like. The real need is to get the right balance between functional expertise and generalist knowledge.

EVALUATING TRAINING AND DEVELOPMENT

Evaluating the effectiveness of training and development is far from straightforward and is especially difficult in the case of management development. Whereas it may be relatively easy to measure increased output on a production line, it is less easy to measure improved administrative efficiency or better customer relations, and virtually impossible to demonstrate improved managerial competence. However, it is still important to try to ensure that any training and development provided is achieving what it is intended to achieve.

The evaluation of training can be carried out at various levels. Hamblin[9] suggests the following:

- *Reactions level* — reviewing the trainees' reactions to the training, the trainer, etc.
- *Learning level* — changes in knowledge, skills and attitudes.
- *Job behaviour level* — change in job behaviour.
- *Organization level* — effect on the organization.
- *Ultimate value* — the benefit, primarily to the organization but also to the individual.

The key consideration is probably the return to the organization, but this can be somewhat difficult to measure. However, training planners cannot just rely on favourable reactions from trainees since it is possible, and not uncommon, to enjoy a course yet learn nothing of practical value from it. On the other hand, if reactions are unfavourable that clearly indicates a fundamental problem to be resolved.

There are a number of ways of assessing the results of training. These include:

- Pre- and post-course questionnaires to test increases in knowledge.
- Observation of the trainees while on the training programme and of their behaviour on return from it.
- Tests of various kinds including possibly the use of assessment centres.
- Interviewing trainees.
- Measured changes in performance, particularly in terms of delivery against targets set as part of a performance management process.

Whatever process of evaluation is used it should seek to ensure that any changes observed are as a result of the training and not for some other, unrelated reason. Ideally, therefore, the evaluation process should be carefully designed, possibly even with the use of a control group, although time and cost constraints probably make such comprehensive studies impractical for most organizations.

References

1   Megginson, D, Joy-Matthews, J and Banfield, P (1993) *Human Resource Development*, Kogan Page, London.

2   Manpower Services Commission (1981) *Glossary of Training Terms*, 3rd edn, HMSO, London.

3   *ibid.*

4   Armstrong, M (1991) *A Handbook of Personnel Management Practice*, 4th edn, Kogan Page, London.

5   Arkin, A (1994) 'The Rolls Royce of Development,' *Personnel Management*, January.

6   Lee, G and Beard, D (1994) *Development Centres*, McGraw Hill, Maidenhead.

7   Revans, R W (1971) *Developing Effective Managers*, Longman, Harlow.

8   Shuttleworth, T and Prescott, R (1991) 'The hard graft way to develop managers', *Personnel Management*, November.

9   Hamblin, A C (1974) *Evaluation and Control of Training*, McGraw-Hill, Maidenhead.

7

Job Evaluation

This chapter examines how the relative size of jobs can be assessed in an organization. Usually the main, although not the only, reason for doing this is to determine the appropriate rate of pay. However, when reading Chapter 8 on reward management it needs to be borne in mind that the determination of internal relativities is normally achieved through some form of job evaluation.

The purpose of job evaluation is to compare all the jobs in the organization, one with another, with the aim of producing a rank order. This rank order may then be subdivided into groups of jobs of the same size, which can, if desired, be placed within pay ranges or grades. While this approach is clearly more appropriate to large organizations, even in small organizations judgements have to be made about how one job compares with another, otherwise no decision can be made about relative pay and status. So, in effect, even where there is no formal method of job evaluation, jobs are evaluated in any case. It is really a question of how analytical the organization wants to be.

Job evaluation is part of the organization's human resource planning process. Once the overall strategy and objectives have been determined, and the structure has been developed, the next step is to establish the required level of human resources, ie to get the right people with the right skills in the right place at the right time. This in turn means having effective selection processes and all the necessary systems to ensure the retention and motivation of staff. Part of this process will inevitably involve deciding on the relative size of jobs, if for no other reason than to ensure that pay is at a level that will attract people and, more importantly, that those within the organization will feel that bigger jobs receive bigger rewards. The main stages in the evaluation process are summarized in Figure 7.1.

Figure 7.1 *The main stages in the job evaluation process*

PRINCIPLES OF JOB EVALUATION

Definition

Pritchard and Murlis[1] define job evaluation as: 'a process for judging the relative size or importance of jobs within an organization'. There are a number of implications and principles underlying this definition.

Job evaluation is a process

Job evaluation is a systematic method or process, as opposed to an approach that is random or non-systematic. This means that jobs are considered against the same criteria in each case, which should ensure consistency. The alternative is a non-analytical approach in which each job is considered in isolation and against what may be entirely different considerations in each case. In such a situation it is not possible to make objective comparisons between jobs and the final judgements are likely to be inconsistent.

Job evaluation is judgemental

Job evaluation is sometimes perceived and described as scientific. This it most definitely is not. In any job evaluation scheme, no matter how sophisticated, where a job is placed in relation to another is a matter of judgement on the part of the evaluators. It certainly should be systematic, however, and make judgements about jobs using common standards. If individuals are left to judge job size without these guidelines the result is that different standards and criteria are likely to be used and it will be like trying to compare eggs with apples.

It is important to remember that job evaluation is one of the processes to help manage the organization and that the intention is to achieve the maximum objectivity.

It is about the relative size of jobs

Job evaluation is a comparative process and ultimately the aim is to compare one job with another. Allocating points to a particular job is an indication of the size of that job in relation to others in that organization, based on the particular criteria contained in the job evaluation method used. Although some job evaluation schemes do facilitate comparisons between organizations, the key measure is one of internal relativity.

Jobs not people

Central to the principles of job evaluation is that it is about jobs, not people. When jobs are being evaluated the evaluators have to forget the individuals doing them and concentrate on the content of the jobs alone. This means that a high performer will not gain additional points or extra credit just for being good at his or her job. Similarly, the individual whose performance falls short of the standard required will not be penalized.

The question is often raised about the person who is undertaking more than may be strictly required in his or her job. Obviously people do change the content of jobs and someone who is highly experienced may well take on additional responsibilities that may not originally have been part of the job. In these circumstances, if the new responsibilities have become a recognized part of the job (which means that they should be reflected in any job description) then they can be evaluated. However, if they are under-taken voluntarily and are not seen as an essential part of the job (which means that any new postholder would presumably not be required to carry them out) they do not form part of the job for evaluation purposes.

In similar vein, if someone is not carrying out the full range of respon-sibilities, the job will still be evaluated as though he or she were, although there might be an issue about performance which could have training or disciplinary implications.

Based on fully satisfactory performance

Implicit in the above is that the evaluation of any job should be based on an assumption of fully satisfactory performance, or performance to the 100 per cent level. Any evaluation that did not take account of the full range of responsibilities required (whether or not they are actually carried out) would not reflect the true importance of the job to the organization.

For the same reason evaluation should not, ideally, take too much account of the consequences of error. In some jobs, serious errors can result in death or destruction or the financial collapse of a company. However, to start taking account of the most serious consequences that can occur if an individual really messes things up is a very slippery slope. Individual postholders can be quite ingenious in thinking up the most appalling disaster scenarios. We have to assume that such disastrous and career-limiting performance is fortunately exceptional, and that generally people can be relied on to perform to the 100 per cent level. Provided they do so, the systems of the organization should be sufficiently robust to prevent disaster. Consider trying to evaluate jobs like that of a nurse or an air traffic controller on any other basis.

Some job evaluation schemes do take account of factors such as pres-sure. However, this is again somewhat risky as it is a very subjective factor. Some people find staff management a burden whereas others thrive on it. Some experience stress through having too much work and others through having too little. Such factors are not objective enough to be part of a robust job evaluation scheme.

Activity — Factors affecting job size

Consider your own job:
1. What are the worse consequences that could arise from a serious error?
2. How likely is this?
3. Do you think that this should be taken into account in considering the size of your job?
4. How much pressure is there in your job?
5. Does everyone cope with pressure equally well?
6. Should the pressure in the job be one of the factors taken into account when evaluating it?

It must be based on good job information

The quality of any evaluation will be crucially dependent on the quality of the job information supplied. For this reason any organization carrying out a job evaluation exercise must ensure that a comprehensive job analysis precedes it, which usually means preparing accurate job descriptions. Job analysis is considered in detail in Chapter 3.

The job as it is today

Inevitably, jobs change over time. However, the evaluation should not take account of changes that are anticipated but have not yet occurred, as they may not actually happen. Often jobs are evaluated when an internal reorganization looks likely to affect the accountabilities of a particular post, and the suggestion is often then made that the evaluation should take account of those changes. The correct approach, however, is either to evaluate the job as it stands and evaluate it again when the changes have been implemented, or to conduct a provisional evaluation of the new job and confirm it later. Alternatively, the evaluation could be deferred until the changes have taken place.

By the same token, any responsibilities that were once part of the job, but are no longer, should be disregarded.

Present grade or salary is irrelevant

Obviously any process which bases the evaluation results on the existing grade or pay structure defeats the whole purpose of conducting the exercise. The existing arrangements may be very unsatisfactory.

In any job evaluation exercise a proportion of jobs will go up in grade or pay terms, some will go down, and some will stay the same. The exact proportions will vary from organization to organization, with those that have more actively managed their pay relativities having fewer overall changes.

TYPES OF JOB EVALUATION SCHEME

Job evaluation schemes divide broadly into analytical and non-analytical schemes[2]. Non-analytical schemes are ranking, paired comparison and classification. These and the analytical methods are considered further below.

Ranking

Ranking compares each job with every other job and places them in order of importance to the organization. Evaluators compare whole jobs rather than the separate components of jobs, but may make these comparisons on the basis of one or more key factors, such as the decisions made or the accountabilities of each post.

The advantages of ranking are simplicity and speed and it may be perfectly adequate for a small organization. However, it has a number of disadvantages:

- Its lack of sophistication means that it may be difficult to defend the results as there will be no way of demonstrating any analysis.
- There can be no guarantee that bias has not been built into the system.
- The lack of objective criteria is likely to mean that judgements made about jobs are inconsistent.
- It is difficult to compare very different jobs for which different aptitudes might be required.
- While a rank order can be obtained the magnitude of the difference between jobs cannot be measured.
- It does not easily enable jobs to be grouped for grading or pay purposes.
- The rationale behind the decisions cannot easily be communicated and the approach is therefore likely to lack credibility with staff.

Paired comparisons

The paired comparisons method of job evaluation is similar to ranking in that complete jobs are compared with all other jobs. However, in this case scores are allocated in terms of whether a particular job is as important, more important or less important than another. In this way, by giving points to each job in turn on the basis of these comparisons, a rank order may be produced.

This approach again has the advantages of simplicity and speed, and correlation of results can be made even faster by the use of a computer. Again it may be perfectly adequate for a small organization. Although it is a slightly more sophisticated way of comparing jobs it suffers from all of the disadvantages of ranking, plus the fact that as the number of jobs increases so do the number of comparisons that have to be made and the calculations involved.

Job classification

Job classification involves the identification of a number of classes or grades of employee, each of which will have certain characteristics, into which all jobs with these characteristics can be placed. Frequently organizations have a grading structure into which jobs are placed on a felt-fair basis but without any detailed analysis of their size. Such systems are very common in the public sector and in large, highly structured organizations.

Job classification again has the advantages of speed and simplicity, but with the added advantage that there are clear grade or job family definitions which enable jobs to be more accurately allocated to the appropriate grade or class.

The main disadvantages of classification are as follows:

- It compares job descriptions with grade criteria, rather than jobs with jobs, which is a less reliable way of getting a rank order.
- It can be difficult to grade more complex jobs.
- The grade definitions may be difficult to formulate and may not always be helpful when allocating jobs to grades.
- There is no easy way of justifying why a job has been allocated a particular grade.
- It is not usually accepted as being a valid approach in equal value cases, ie those in which a claim is made that a certain job or type of work is equal in value to that undertaken by a member of the opposite sex and should therefore receive equal pay.
- There is no guarantee that bias has not been built into the process.
- This approach can be subject to grade drift whereby, over time, the grades of various jobs will tend to creep up, usually depending on the advocacy skills of the manager seeking any increase.
- It can result in the introduction of too many grades and job categories, which in turn can have implications for the organization structure and will complicate pay policy.

Points rating

Points rating or points factor rating consists of the identification of a number of factors considered to be relevant to all the jobs under consideration and allocation of points to the different levels of these factors. Jobs are then compared against each of these factors and points given accordingly, and then the separate factors are totalled to give an overall score.

Once all the jobs have been evaluated the organization will have a rank order of scores which can then be further divided into grades against which pay levels can be set. There are numerous examples of such schemes and a number of factors which commonly occur, such as knowledge and experience, decisions made, complexity, etc. Such schemes may be bought 'off-the-shelf' or can be designed specifically for the organization in question. The main advantages of using an off-the-shelf scheme are that it saves a lot of the time required to design a bespoke scheme and it will have been tried and tested in other organizations. The main drawback is that the factors may not be entirely appropriate to the jobs in the organization or may not reflect the organization's culture.

The main steps involved in introducing a tailor-made scheme are as follows:

1. Identify the factors to be applied — by analysing a representative sample of jobs from various levels and functions to decide which are the factors that differentiate them.
2. Allocate points and weightings to these factors and describe a number of levels (see example in Figure 7.2).
3. Identify a sample of jobs about which there is agreement on the rank order, usually described as 'benchmark' jobs.
4. Test the points and weightings against this sample.
5. Fine tune the results until the points produce the expected results.
6. Ideally, test these results against a wider sample.
7. Again, fine tune the results.
8. Evaluate the remaining posts in the organization.

Points schemes have the advantages and disadvantages outlined in Table 7.1.

Factor comparison

Factor comparison differs from points rating in that jobs are compared

Table 7.1 *Advantages and disadvantages of points schemes*

Advantages	Disadvantages
As evaluators have to consider each job in terms of a number of factors they are able to be more objective in their judgements.	Their analytical nature can give a spurious impression of scientific accuracy, when in fact they are still dependent on evaluators' judgements.
Because all jobs are being considered against the same criteria there is likely to be greater consistency in the judgements made.	They can be expensive and time consuming to install and maintain.
Evaluators are able to demonstrate analytical reasons for making particular judgements about jobs.	They are based on an assumption that all the factors used are equally relevant to all jobs, which may not be the case.
The allocation of points makes the process of developing a grade structure or pay bands easier.	
The size of the difference between jobs can be measured.	
The system is more likely to be perceived as fair than one in which the criteria are not known.	
The approach is more likely to be accepted in equal value cases.	
Such schemes are relatively easy to computerize.	

People skills

Knowledge and experience	1 Politeness and courtesy only required	2 Requires some verbal and/or written communication skills	3 Requires good verbal and written communication skills or has to exercise a high level of tact and discretion	4 Has to exercise significant persuasive skills because the post involves a high degree of motivation, selling or negotiation	5 Requires persuasive or motivational skills of the highest order as the post will be involved in discussions crucial to the success of the Institute
A Basic education only — no previous work experience required	50	60	72	86	103
B Basic education plus some specialized skills gained through experience	60	72	86	103	124
C GCSE level or relevant experience	72	86	103	124	149
D GCE 'A' level or relevant experience	86	103	124	149	179

Figure 7.2 *An extract from a tailor-made job evaluation scheme*

with each other on a number of different factors rather than as whole jobs. This produces several different hierarchies of jobs as some will be high on some factors but low on others. Comparisons are made of the lists of factor rankings and judgements made about how much of each job is attributable to each factor, eg the percentage of the job's total size which might relate to a factor covering responsibility.

While this approach is analyical and objective it is relatively little used because it is time consuming, complex and costly to install.

Other methods

Over the years a variety of approaches to job evaluation have been developed. A number of these have concentrated on a single factor rather than a range of factors. Examples of these include the Time Span of Discretion method, developed by Elliott Jaques and applied at Glacier Metals in the 1950s and 1960s, and decision banding.

The former is based on the assumption that work contains two components: '(a) the discretionary element, comprising the discretion, choice or judgement which the person doing the work is expected to exercise; and (b) the prescribed content, comprising the rules, regulations, procedures and policies, the custom and practice, and the physical limits of plant, equipment or tooling, which set external limits within which the discretion has to be exercised'.[3] The hypothesis was that factor (a) correlated with the difficulty of the job and could therefore be used as a measure of job size.

Decision banding allocates jobs to bands based on the level of decisions made, eg from policy-making decisions to tightly prescribed decisions only about methods of working.

These other methods tended originally to concentrate on the outputs from jobs, no doubt arising from the principles of the scientific management movement. Lately, however, there has been more emphasis on input factors such as the skills or competencies required to carry out a particular job. The reality is that virtually any job will be a combination of both, plus throughput factors, ie the thinking process. It seems logical therefore that any job evaluation scheme should have all these different elements built in. Some factors affecting the size of jobs are illustrated in Figure 7.3.

Computerized job evaluation

The criticisms made of job evaluation are considered later in this chapter. However, one of the most common of these is the time taken to install and maintain any job evaluation system. One way round this problem is the use of computerized methods of job evaluation and a number of such schemes have been devised, including those developed by Hay, KPMG and Reference Point. HM Treasury uses a scheme known as JEGS — Job Evaluation Grading Support — developed by Towers Perrin, which automatically evaluates jobs following completion of a detailed job analysis questionnaire, an approach common to most such systems[4]. Herein lies the main

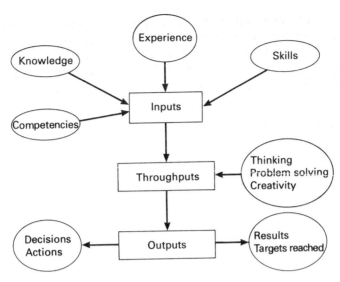

Figure 7.3 *Factors affecting the size of jobs*

difficulty. Getting the design of the questionnaire right is absolutely crucial and it can be a surprisingly lengthy and complex process. This is especially so when applied to different countries and cultures, and certain international companies have spent considerable time and effort designing culturally sound questionnaires. Once implemented, however, subsequent evaluation and maintenance should be much less time consuming than with other approaches. Time will tell.

> **Activity — Job evaluation in your organization**
> 1. How are jobs evaluated in your organization?
> 2. What are the strengths of the approach used?
> 3. What are the weaknesses?
> 4. If job evaluation is not used, how is pay determined?

COMMUNICATION

It is very important to ensure that a job evaluation exercise is effectively communicated to employees. Precisely what is communicated and in how much detail is something that has to be carefully considered. As a minimum, the employees should be:

- ■ told that a job evaluation exercise is to take place;
- ■ informed of the aims and objectives of the exercise;
- ■ notified of the process and the timescale involved;
- ■ informed of the scheme principles;

■   notified about the results of the exercise, although the amount of detail they are given will vary from organization to organization.

In notifying employees about the results of the exercise the question is often raised about whether individuals should be told the actual number of points allocated to their particular job (if it is a points rating scheme). Certainly they will need to be told the grade or pay range allocated. Frequently they are also notified of the points range into which all jobs of that size fall, eg grade 6 = 200–250 points. The danger with telling someone that his or her job scored a specific number of points is that if it is near a grade boundary there will be a strong temptation to appeal against the result (if there is an appeal process). It is also difficult to be totally confident that any precise number of points is correct, whereas evaluators can be more confident that a job falls within a particular range. The organization's policy on this will depend on its culture and history.

Of course, job evaluation can be used solely as a management tool without the employees being involved, in which case communication will be kept to the minimum. However, it must be remembered that their cooperation will be required to obtain accurate job information.

Wherever possible the cooperation of the trade unions should be obtained and they should be involved in the process. In this way they are more likely to buy into the result, rather than oppose it.

OBTAINING JOB INFORMATION

The accuracy of the results from any job evaluation exercise is crucially dependent on accurate job information. Generally the main sources of such information are interviews with postholders or job descriptions. In large organizations, because of the time and cost of interviewing large numbers of staff, the more common source is the job description. This is usually completed by the postholder, who knows the job better than anyone, and it is then approved by his or her manager. However, where a post is vacant, or where the individual has only recently been appointed, the line manager may be the most appropriate source of information.

Supplementary information is also likely to be required from organization charts, any business plan, etc.

JOB EVALUATION PANELS

Although jobs can be evaluated by an individual it is more common in organizations of any size to have a job evaluation panel. This reduces the danger of individual bias, as everyone has prejudices about the worth of particular jobs and these will be diluted by a group process. It also gives access to a wider range of knowledge about the organization and its jobs, and is generally perceived to be fairer.

Panel or committee members should be people who have sound judgement and credibility within the organization. It is also useful to try to ensure that as wide a range of job types as possible can be covered by the group's combined knowledge. Similarly, the panel should be representative of the organization's employees. For example, if there are no women evaluators the process may be discriminatory, even if the scheme itself is free of any such bias. However, the panel should also be kept as small as possible, otherwise it becomes unwieldy and might involve too much time and resources.

Decisions should be by consensus. If there is no agreement this is likely to mean that the evaluators do not understand the job and require more information or clarification.

APPEALS

A frequently asked question is whether the organization should have an appeal process. This really depends on the culture of the organization and whether job evaluation is being conducted just as a management exercise. If it is the latter, then it is unlikely that an appeal process would make any sense. However, in many large organizations with a history of joint consultation, it may be very difficult to avoid such a process.

Where an appeal process is introduced the question arises as to what employees are to be permitted to appeal against, and how much information they should be given. Appeals can be against the job evaluation score, the grade allocated or the pay given. While the last two items may be a reasonable subject of appeal, appeals against the score should generally be resisted as the individual is unlikely to know how the score has been arrived at unless he or she has been trained in the job evaluation methodology. In practice this could mean having to train everyone, which would make little sense. As an alternative, however, some employee representatives could be trained.

The organization should make it clear what will be accepted as a basis for an appeal, mere dissatisfaction with the result being an inadequate reason. This will determine how much information is given.

The final consideration is who should hear the appeal. Generally, it should be people who were not involved in making the original decision, although they must of course be trained in the evaluation methodology.

CRITICISMS OF JOB EVALUATION

A number of criticisms are often made of job evaluation, and some are explored below.

Job evaluation is time consuming and bureaucratic

It can be. Some organizations fall into the trap of being seduced by the

---

Case study — Job evaluation in a county council

Many local authorities have introduced job evaluation in recent years. This particular example covers the introduction of the Hay Guide Chart and Profile Method, which is the most widely used. The process involved some typical stages:

■ Deciding the scope of the exercise — in this case all jobs, numbering several thousand.
■ Deciding the process, including such issues as evaluation panel membership, how to collect job data, union involvement, what to communicate to staff, etc.
■ Identifying benchmark jobs, meaning in this context a representative sample of different levels and types of jobs.
■ Obtaining job data through structured questionnaires.
■ Training evaluators.
■ Evaluating the benchmark jobs.
■ Reviewing the benchmark evaluations to look for anomalies — a process decribed by Hay as 'sore-thumbing'.
■ Evaluating remaining posts.
■ Again reviewing results as described above.
■ Production of grade structure and pay recommendations.

This process produced some difficulties typical of this kind of exercise. These included suspicion on the part of large numbers of staff about the reasons for the exercise, similar suspicion on the part of the unions with some added ideological reservations, and strong interdepartmental rivalry. Usually if unions are built into the process any initial suspicion disappears and they become enthusiastic evaluators, which is indeed what happened. The interdepartmental rivalry was more difficult to overcome and manifested itself by council officers seeking to try to boost the evaluation scores for their own departments. This of course defeats the purpose of the exercise and was overcome in this case by having fairly constituted and representative evaluation panels and by applying consistent standards for comparable levels of job.

Other issues arising that you may wish to consider are:

1. How much detail about the results of the exercise should be given to staff — total points awarded or just final grade or salary?
2. What protection should be given to jobs downgraded?
3. Should there be an appeal process?
4. If large numbers of posts are upgraded, how can implementation costs be kept under control?
5. How should the system be maintained?

---

process and tend to forget that it is only a means to an end. Large evaluation panels meeting for days on end to consider just a few jobs can tend to become talking shops or a battleground on which long-held grievances are paraded.

Panels should be kept small and be effectively chaired. Where possible evaluation data should be computerized to speed up processing and data management.

It is unnecessary

In some organizations it is. Some are too small to justify an analytical scheme. Other organizations are totally dominated by the market rate and have to pay whatever is necessary to attract people. Most organizations, however, try to put some kind of value on their jobs. The question is only how well they do it.

It is subjective

Job evaluation can never be completely objective as judgements about jobs will tend to incorporate individual and organizational prejudices. However, it is more objective than 'gut feel'.

Fragmenting pay markets mean that it has lost relevance

It is certainly true that different pay markets can be identified for different types of job. However, it is still important for the organization to maintain internal equity and to have one overall and consistent pay policy for all jobs. Market differences can be reflected by the payment of differentials for certain employee groups.

It cannot reflect the flexibility now required in jobs

It can, provided that flexibility is reflected in the description of the job requirements. In effect this means writing job descriptions in terms of wide accountabilities and objectives.

It undervalues individual performance

Job evaluation only looks at job size. Postholders should also be subject to a comprehensive performance management process.

It is costly to maintain

It can be, but there a number of job evaluation schemes in existence that require relatively little maintenance and are therefore cost effective.

Ownership is by the personnel department not line managers

A study by Industrial Relations Services found that one of the criticisms of job evaluation was that, because the process was complex, it remained in the ownership of the personnel department. This is an important criticism as it really needs to be owned by managers to maintain credibility. Processes therefore should be developed that can be applied by managers without the requirement for specialist personnel knowledge.

References

[1] Pritchard, D and Murlis, H (1992) *Jobs, Roles and People*, Nicholas Brealey Publishing, London.

[2] Armstrong, M and Murlis, H (1992) *Reward Management*, 2nd edn, Kogan Page, London.

[3] Jaques, E (1961) *Equitable Payment*, Heinemann, Oxford.

[4] *Industrial Relations Review and Report No. 551*, Eclipse Group Ltd, January 1994.

8

Pay and Benefits

This chapter concerns the issue of pay and benefits, or reward, as it is commonly described. The organization's reward strategy is a key component of its corporate strategy, not least because the costs of employing staff are likely to be one of the biggest items on the balance sheet. However, there is more to it than that. What is often overlooked is that the way in which employees are rewarded in terms of their pay and benefits sends powerful messages to them and, for that matter, to the shareholders and public in general.

All elements of reward, and this includes non-financial rewards as well as the financial ones that are the subject of this chapter, are part of the employer's contract with the employee. The employee agrees to perform a certain job in return for some kind of reward. Rewards in the wider sense can include such other elements as promotion prospects, training opportunities and job satisfaction, etc, and these all play a part in attracting, retaining and motivating staff of the right calibre. The emphasis here is on the strategies, systems and processes needed to achieve these aims.

The place of reward in relation to the other aspects of human resource management is summarized in Figure 8.1.

PRINCIPLES OF REWARD STRATEGY

Armstrong and Murlis[1] state that reward strategies must:

- be congruent with and support corporate values and beliefs;
- emanate from business strategy and goals;
- be linked to organization performance;
- drive and support desired behaviour at all levels;
- fit the desired management style;
- provide the competitive edge needed to attract and retain the high level of skills the organization needs;
- be anchored to the realities of the labour market.

These criteria summarize what the organization wants from its reward

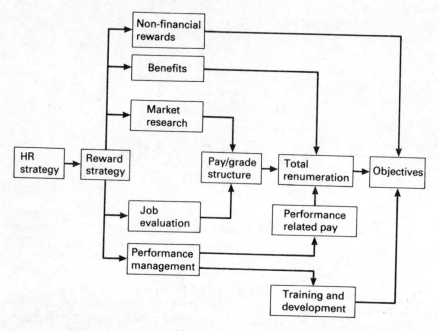

Figure 8.1 *The reward management process*
Source: Adapted from Hay Management Consultants

strategy. The other side of the coin is what the individual employee expects. Individual aims and expectations will differ, but most people would probably agree that they are looking for one or more of the following:

- a 'fair' day's pay for a 'fair' day's work;
- a reward system which is seen to allocate rewards fairly;
- some link between the individual's contribution to the organization and the rewards received;
- rewards in line with those that are paid to do similar jobs in other organizations;
- particularly in managerial and professional jobs, some form of progression in pay;
- certain minimum benefits, eg most employees would expect paid holidays, sickness pay and a pension.

Provided the aims of the organization and the expectations of the employees can be integrated, the reward strategy can be a powerful mechanism in the implementation of the organization's human resource strategy. It can:

- reinforce the aims and objectives of the organization and ensure that employee behaviour is directed to their attainment;
- give clear messages about the organization's culture and values, particularly in terms of what behaviours and actions are valued;

- help to motivate employees;
- attract and retain employees of the required calibre;
- provide rewards for particular effort or high performance, and encourage high-flyers;
- send messages about unacceptable performance;
- establish priorities for individual postholders;
- encourage innovative and strategic thinking;
- encourage a focus on those issues considered vital to business success;
- encourage efficiency, effectiveness and high productivity.

DEFINITIONS

Reward management covers salaries, wages and benefits. To understand these fully it is first necessary to define some of the most common terms used in reward management generally and in this chapter particularly. These key definitions are set out below.

Base salary

The base salary is the contractually agreed rate for a job. It is the amount the individual can expect to receive on a regular basis regardless of performance.

Total cash

Total cash is the amount of basic pay plus any variable elements, such as bonuses or profit related pay which the individual can expect to receive. It is the total amount of cash actually paid.

Total remuneration

Total remuneration refers to the total value of the reward package, including the value put on any benefits.

Differences between salaries and wages

Differences arose between salaries and wages because of differences in the nature of work undertaken. In the past, and in manufacturing environments in particular, there was always a clear distinction between production operatives, the manual and craft employees who were actually engaged in the manufacturing process, and managerial and professional staff who administered the organization. This distinction still holds good today, although the differences are less marked and there has been a growth in white-collar employment with a corresponding decline in blue-collar work. Originally, the employment of manual and craft employees could be varied with the production requirements of the company, so they might be employed for a week or two and then laid off to fit in with fluctuations in demand. Indeed, the requirement could even be for employment just for a number of hours. Consequently such employees tended to be hourly paid.

While wages tend to be a fixed hourly or weekly rate, with time and a half and double time being paid for overtime, weekend and holiday working, and with additional productivity bonuses, salaries are usually an annual figure paid monthly, generally with no additions for productivity or overtime, provided the employee has reached a certain level in the organization.

Generally the differences between salaries and wages have now been eroded and there is a trend to what is called harmonization, in which all employees are employed on the same conditions of service. There are, however, a number of complexities in harmonization, primarily because of the number of allowances that have tended to be added to basic wages, often negotiated by the trade unions. These include unsocial hours payments, attendance bonuses, tool allowances and dirty money (paid when employees are required to undertake particularly unpleasant tasks), plus the overtime and productivity bonuses mentioned. On the other hand, white-collar staff have traditionally enjoyed a range of benefits not available to blue-collar employees, such as pensions or private health care.

Benefits

Benefits are non-cash additions to basic pay. The reasons for paying benefits are:

- to attract and retain staff of the right calibre, as there is a certain expectation from employees and prospective employees about the kinds of benefits that go with a particular type of job and organization;
- to ensure that the organization is able to compete for staff on an equal footing with other organizations paying benefits;
- to promote the welfare of staff and to maintain their level of satisfaction with and commitment to the organization;
- to meet the actual and perceived needs of employees;
- to provide a tax-efficient form of remuneration;
- to demonstrate to the world that the employer is a caring one.

DEVELOPING A REWARD STRATEGY

There are a number of stages to go through in developing a reward strategy for an organization. In addition to bearing in mind the principles outlined above, the organization should:

- be clear about the aims of the reward strategy;
- have a clear idea about the numbers, levels and types of staff required as determined by the human resource planning process;
- decide on what it values and therefore what it is prepared to pay for;
- take account of any existing recruitment and retention difficulties;

■ decide what can be afforded;
■ take account of internal and external relativities.

Clear aims

The organization's management should be clear about what it is they are seeking to achieve in their reward strategy. This should generally relate back to the business plan. For example, if a company wants to increase its market share, one way of reinforcing this message is to give managers bonuses for achieving any such increase. In a wider context, if the aim is to attract the very best talent then the company will have to pay premium rates. Such is the case particularly with so-called gold-collar workers such as top professional footballers. If the organization is seeking stability it may wish to introduce policies which tie employees to it, such as subsidized mortgages and generous pensions.

Linkage with the human resource planning process

This and the previous item are inextricably linked since the human resource planning process will need to relate closely to the organization's aims and objectives. If the organization is going for growth this leads to a quite different configuration of jobs and people than if it is retrenching or contracting. In the former case there is likely to be a need to recruit new talent, particularly if a company is expanding into new markets. In some cases this may be through acquisition or merger, which brings its own problems of assimilating different pay and working practices, whereas in others it may be through the usual selection channels.

Whatever the organization's position there needs to be clarity about the types of job required, usually gained through an analysis of the deliverables expected, the type of person required to fill the job, ie a personnel specification, the numbers required to deliver the service to the desired standards and the reward packages likely to attract people of the right calibre.

Taking account of organization values

In deciding pay policy one of the first questions that should be asked is what the organization wants to pay for. This is less obvious than it might seem. A knee-jerk reaction might be that the organization wants to pay for high performance, but the issue is really more complex. Most managements would probably accept that the bigger the job, the more it should be paid. However, this raises issues about what is meant by job size and how it can be assessed. Where job evaluation is used to determine job size (see Chapter 7), the factors chosen and the weightings given to different jobs will affect their position in the hierarchy and consequently the grade or rate of pay.

In some markets and for some jobs it is likely to be the going rate, ie whatever the organization has to pay to attract staff of the right calibre, that determines the pay policy. In this case job size is likely to be a secondary consideration.

Difficulties can arise where there is a conflict between job size and the market rate. One local authority employed archaeologists. Because the supply outstrips demand the authority was able to recruit all the staff it needed with the required qualifications without having to pay premium rates. However, because a job evaluation scheme introduced by the council placed a high value on the knowledge requirements of jobs, these posts scored higher than many of those that were traditionally graded higher. The question was whether the council should apply the principles of the job evaluation scheme or follow the dictates of the market. Similar considerations frequently arise about other groups, such as accountants and lawyers, who are generally paid at the upper end of the jobs market and often have to be paid some kind of market supplement to reflect this.

Of course questions of job size are only about the job. The other significant consideration is the performance of the individual in the job and whether the organization thinks it should pay for this. To do so opens up a whole raft of other issues which are examined in more detail in Chapter 5 on performance management.

Recruitment and retention difficulties

The ability of the organization to attract and retain staff of the right calibre will clearly affect the reward strategy. While high turnover does not necessarily mean that the organization is not competitive in terms of reward, that could be one of the factors. Similarly, the fact that nobody has left for some time does not mean that everything in the garden is rosy. It might just mean that in recessionary times people are much more careful about changing jobs and fewer jobs are available. It could also mean that the organization is paying more than it needs to.

What can be afforded

It is self-evident that no organization should pay more than it can afford. However, paying at the bottom of the market is likely to mean a consequently low standard of staff (except in those traditionally low-paying occupations and sectors which rely on the vocational attitudes and goodwill of staff). On the other hand, paying at the top of the market means that the organization has got to get top-level performance.

Taking account of internal and external relativities

The organization has to take account of the relative position of jobs internally as well as relationships with market comparators. Of the two, it is probably the internal relativities that are the more crucial. Little upsets employees more than the thought that someone who they feel is doing a lesser job is nevertheless being paid more. It is therefore important to establish these relativities at an early stage, preferably by using some form of analytical job evaluation if the organization is of significant size. Approaches to job evaluation are described in Chapter 7.

If external relativities are wrong there is a danger that the organization may lose staff to competitors. One of the main questions in this context is which the appropriate comparators are. These will vary between industries, functions, jobs and locations. For senior management jobs the market is likely to be a national one, whereas for clerical and secretarial staff it is more likely to be local to the organization. The way to determine these external relativities is through surveys, which can be purchased off-the-shelf or bespoke, ie conducted specifically for the organization, and through reviewing job advertisements, although these may often exaggerate the salaries actually paid.

Finally, once the market data has been obtained the organization has to decide where it wants to be in the market. If it decides to be somewhere near the top of the pay market then it must be sure of getting a correspondingly high level of performance to justify the higher pay bill. On the other hand, if it decides to be near the lower end of the market it may have difficulty in attracting and retaining staff of the right calibre. While this may be a position that can be held during a recession, there is a danger that as soon as conditions improve people will seek better paid jobs.

REWARD STRUCTURES

A reward structure is the way in which the organization pays its employees. This can be some kind of salary scale or grade applied to different categories and groups in the organization or it might be a single salary point or wage paid to one particular job. Armstrong and Murlis[2] identify seven main types of reward structure:

1. Graded salary structure.
2. Individual job range.
3. Progression or pay curves related to competency levels.
4. Job family system.
5. Spot rates.
6. Pay spine.
7. Rate for age.

Graded salary structures

A graded salary structure consists of a number of pay ranges or grades, each with a specified maximum and minimum and through which an individual postholder will progress on the basis of experience, performance or length of service. Jobs are allocated to grades according to their size, with broadly comparable jobs being placed within the same grade.

Such structures can have a number of fixed points or increments that individuals progress to on the basis of pre-determined criteria, or may give flexibility to apply any salary within the range. The size of the range can vary considerably and can be defined either in terms of the percentage increase between the highest and lowest points or as a percentage of the mid-point. A 20–40 per cent difference between the maximum and the minimum is quite common, although other range widths can also be used. In the public sector range widths traditionally tend to be narrower and are usually comprised of a number of set increments. The number of different grades will depend on the number of job types and levels in the organization structure.

The wider the pay range, the greater the degree of overlap between the maximum of one grade and the minimum of the next. This has implications for the way the pay policy is managed. The extent to which a high-performing subordinate may be allowed to earn more than a less effective superior will depend on the culture of the organization and the effectiveness of its performance management processes.

An example of a pay range is given in Table 8.1, and a diagram of an overlapping grade structure in Figure 8.2. Generally the mid-point of the range may be regarded as the rate for the job, ie the salary the organization would expect to pay for a job of that size.

Progression through the grade can be based on a number of different factors but usually depends either on performance or service. Where it is based on performance, the individual's position in the grade will normally be reviewed towards the year end and be based on the performance rating achieved. Where service is the key determinant the individual will progress automatically through the grade over time, usually by fixed increments. While this used to be a very common approach, especially in the public sector, its popularity is waning as more employers seek to relate progress to performance. The latter approach means that high performers can be progressed more rapidly.

The main advantages and disadvantages of grades are set out in Table 8.2.

Individual job ranges

Individual job ranges entail the payment of different pay ranges to each individual job, rather than jobs of similar size being grouped together and paid within a common range. These may be appropriate where there are a number of very dissimilar jobs or where the jobs are changing rapidly.

Table 8.1 *Pay range*

	Minimum (£)	Mid-point (£)	Maximum (£)
1	18,000	20,000	22,000
2	22,500	25,000	27,500

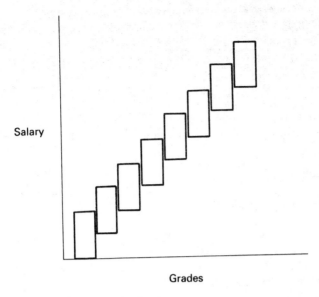

Salary

Grades

Figure 8.2 *An overlapping grade structure*

However, as they will each need to be managed separately, they are really only appropriate where there are a small number of jobs involved, such as for the senior managerial posts in an organization. Their advantages and disadvantages are explained in Table 8.3.

Table 8.2 *Advantages and disadvantages of grades*

Advantages	Disadvantages
Jobs of approximately equal size can be grouped together easily.	They can be inflexible as some jobs may not fit easily into a particular grade and because they restrict exceptions such as rewarding particularly high performance or when a new recruit is earning more than the grade offered.
Starting salaries and progression can be easily controlled thus assisting in salary management.	
Salary planning is easier because there are clear pay boundaries and progression steps.	They can become distorted if certain jobs are paid outside the correct grade because of market rates etc.
It is easier to establish and maintain differentials between jobs.	They can be subject to grade drift, ie the tendency for jobs to be placed in higher grades over time.
They give transparent equity to the pay process, provided there is some analytical means of determining the appropriate grade.	It is difficult to reward staff who reach the top of their grade.
	Overlaps require careful management.

Table 8.3 *Advantages and disadvantages of individual job ranges*

Advantages	Disadvantages
They can give greater flexibility by being tailored to individual jobs.	They require more active management time and administration.
They can be adapted to reflect the demands of the external pay market without upsetting internal pay relativities.	They are less likely to result in a consistent pay policy.
They avoid the problems sometimes associated with allocating jobs to grades.	As numbers increase, they are more difficult to maintain in a consistent and equitable way.

Progression or pay curves

In some environments, especially those with professional or research staff, it may be more difficult to analyse jobs in terms of their size. The actual work undertaken by each jobholder might depend more on the experience and capabilities of that person. Similarly, in this kind of environment what is actually paid may depend more on the market rate for the job in question. In such circumstances it might be appropriate to apply progression curves, in which different pay rates are applied to different levels of competence and to the market rate for that job. The assumption is made that individuals will not progress to a new pay level until they have reached a pre-defined level of competence. The advantages and disadvantages of this approach are laid out in Table 8.4 and an example of a pay curve is shown in Figure 8.3.

Table 8.4 *Advantages and disadvantages of progression or pay curves*

Advantages	Disadvantages
There is flexibility to reward individual performance.	Comparison between jobs is more difficult.
They recognize that competence can increase over time and through greater experience.	Because of the lack of analytical job measurement decisions are more difficult to defend in terms of equal pay for work of equal value.
They do not depend on getting the measurement or evaluation of the job right.	Some competencies and outputs can be difficult to define and measure, making the approach more subjective.
They make it easier to relate different pay markets to different jobs.	Different individual levels of pay make it more difficult to apply a fair and consistent pay policy.
	They could have a demotivating effect if individuals feel they are not being treated fairly in relation to their colleagues.

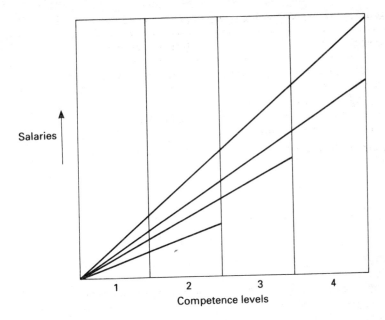

Figure 8.3 *Pay curves*

Job families

Generally any organization should seek to apply a single consistent salary policy and structure. However, where there are a number of distinct groups of staff each with different relevant pay markets, the organization might wish to treat them as separate job families and apply different pay rates. It might be desirable, for example, to distinguish between IT, accountancy, sales, administration and management jobs, all of which could be placed on separate pay scales with different progression rates and criteria. The advantages and disadvantages of this approach are covered in Table 8.5.

Spot rates

A spot rate approach is taken when there is a single pay rate for a particular job. Usually it is based on just one amount being the appropriate pay, but it could also be one point within a range. There is no entitlement to any progression. The vast majority of manual workers are paid on this system. Its advantages and disadvantages are explained in Table 8.6.

Pay spines

Pay spines consist of a series of incremental points extending from the smallest job in the organization to the largest. The spine is then normally divided into grades. Progression is usually automatic and dependent on service. These are more common in the public sector than anywhere else,

Table 8.5 *Advantages and disadvantages of job families*

Advantages	Disadvantages
The organization is able to take account of different pay markets for different types of job.	Separate pay structures make an overall consistent pay policy more difficult to apply.
Different progression criteria can be applied.	More research is necessary to ensure that market data is accurate and up to date.
Distortion of the pay structure is avoided.	It is difficult to cross boundaries between different job families which can inhibit flexibility.
	Staff in less well remunerated job families could feel resentful.
	It is difficult to make comparisons of equal value.

and have similar advantages and disadvantages to pay scales, but with the added disadvantage that individuals can just sit tight and progress automatically up their scale, often without having to earn progress through performance.

Rate for age

This is usually an incremental scale linked to age and is based on the assumption that younger employees are on a learning curve and their value to the organization increases with their growth in experience and maturity.

Table 8.6 *Advantages and disadvantages of spot rates*

Advantages	Disadvantages
They can give flexibility and enable the organization to respond quickly to changes.	They can become difficult to administer as organizations increase in size, complexity and the number of different jobs.
They do not create any expectation of pay progression (other than through cost of living increases).	They are based on the assumption that there is a rate for the job, and for many jobs this is not true, particularly for those of an administrative or professional nature.
They may be less divisive than pay scales if everyone in a group is on the same rate.	They lack flexibility as there is no scope for varying the amount that can be offered on promotion or in recognition of increased knowledge and experience.
	They offer no prospects of progression and can therefore be demotivating.

Such an approach has the advantage that it is easy to administer and can be seen to be completely equitable. Its main disadvantage is that it takes no account of performance.

BONUSES AND INCENTIVES

In addition to the base pay many organizations pay bonuses or incentives. Bonuses may be paid for any reason which may not be related to performance, eg an automatic Christmas bonus, whereas incentives are really intended to encourage better performance, although the two terms are often used interchangeably. The types of incentives and bonuses available vary considerably and some of the main ones are described briefly below. More information on relating pay to performance is given in Chapter 5 on performance management.

Productivity payments

In past years there was a strong emphasis in manual and craft jobs on work study based bonus schemes. These schemes, which owe their origins to scientific management principles, sought to break jobs down into their individual components and measure how long each task took. From these results it was possible to produce times for standard performance and calculate bonuses based on achieving and exceeding targets. While such schemes are still common they have declined in popularity in favour of flexibility deals covering working methods, hours, and terms and conditions of employment.

Executive incentive schemes

Executive incentive schemes come in many different forms and it is beyond the scope of this book to consider them in detail. The main aims of such schemes are to:

- raise executives' awareness of the organization's key objectives and encourage a greater focus on these objectives;
- recognize the individual's contribution to the success of the organization;
- enable individuals to share in the organization's success;
- link compensation to organizational performance.

How effective such schemes are at increasing motivation is debateable, since executives are frequently looking for rewards other than money. Kohn[3] has gone so far as to say that 'Rewards secure one thing — temporary compliance. When it comes to producing lasting change in attitudes and behaviour, however, rewards like punishment are strikingly ineffective.' In his view pay is not a motivator (a common stance — see the *Organisational Behaviour and Design* title in this series[4]) and rewards actually punish, because they are manipulative, rupture relationships, ignore reasons, discourage risk taking and undermine interest. However, such schemes do provide a tangible means of giving recognition. Their main danger is that they can quickly demotivate if the rewards are seen as inadequate, and any drop from the previous year can serve to reinforce the message that the organization (or the individual) is not doing so well.

Some of the main considerations when introducing such schemes are as follows:

- What performance measures are to be used? These will usually be a combination of the measurable, eg earnings per share, net profit, sales turnover or return on capital employed, and the more subjective, such as business development or staff motivation.
- How much of pay is to be at risk?
- What level of payments should be made?
- What formula should be used to calculate the payments?
- How frequently should payments be made?
- Who should be included?
- How should any 'windfall' profits be treated?
- How should the incentive be linked to the remuneration package?

Case study — Pay and incentives in a divisionalized structure

A company operating primarily in the retail sector, with six separate business divisions and a turnover of between £300–£400 million, wished to introduce a revised pay and incentives package for its divisional directors, all of whom sat on the group board. The main problem was how to get a common and consistent policy but at the same time take account of the very different business environments in which they operated.

These differences manifested themselves in two main ways. First, some divisions were having an easier time than others because business conditions were more favourable. Secondly, the market rates for jobs varied between the sectors. One sector, for example, traditionally paid lower salaries because there were substantial other benefits available. The company was primarily interested in internal equity but did not feel able to ignore market considerations.

In the event the base pay levels given were a compromise, tending to be driven by the better paid sectors. There was an incentive element of pay, with an additional 15 per cent of salary payable for on-target performance. This was made up of 5 per cent for company performance and 10 per cent related to individual performance. Individual performance measures were different for each director and reflected the business priorities of that particular division.

The main pay issues applying in this company and applicable to others with similar structures are:

- To what extent should you take account of the external pay market when setting pay relativities?
- What incentives should be paid to directors?
- What performance measures should be used?
- How much should be based on company performance and how much on individual performance?
- To what extent should the external business position be taken into account?

BENEFITS

The actual type and level of benefits given will vary between organizations and industry sectors and between jobs. For example, it has been common practice in the financial services sector to give subsidized mortgages, but this is far from common outside that sector. Similarly, company cars given for status reasons, as opposed to necessity, usually only apply at the more senior levels of the organization. The practice also varies between countries, with company cars being comparatively rare in France, for example.

Common benefits

Some of the more common benefits are:

- car;
- pension;
- permanent health insurance;
- personal accident insurance;
- death in service benefits;
- medical insurance;
- holidays;
- relocation expenses;
- enhanced maternity leave;
- paternity leave;
- payment of professional subscriptions;
- payment of telephone bills;
- season ticket loans;
- long service awards;
- other awards;
- subsidized canteen;
- subsidized mortgage;
- sports and social facilities;
- time off, eg for public duties;
- sabbatical leave.

The above list is by no means exhaustive but gives some indication of the range of benefits available. It is beyond the scope of this book to consider these in detail, but Armstrong and Murlis[5] and the *Remuneration and Benefits Handbook*[6] will give further detail if required.

Some issues relating to benefits

Some of the main issues affecting employers in relation to benefits are as follows:

- *Communicating the value of benefits* — very few employees really appreciate just how much the benefits package is worth, representing

Case Study — Unipart

Share options are a benefit normally reserved for directors. However, it is reported' that motor components supplier Unipart is offering shopfloor workers the opportunity to participate in such a scheme.

The scheme would apply to all full-time staff who have worked for the company for over six months, who have received a satisfactory appraisal and whose division reached its 1993 targets. It is estimated that 2600 of the 3800 staff would be eligible. They will be given the option to buy a limited number of shares, 5 or 10 depending on service, at a 15 per cent discount for every one bought at the market rate.

You may wish to consider the following points:

1. How does this scheme compare with typical executive share option schemes?
2. What are the advantages and disadvantages of this approach?
3. Does it penalize those who work for a division that has not reached its targets for reasons that may be beyond an individual's control?

perhaps as much as 25–30 per cent of the total package in some cases, and even more for some senior jobs. In Europe generally this percentage varies from about 20 per cent in Germany to nearer 30 per cent in Belgium. Many employers are missing a trick here, as most fail to communicate to their employees just how much value they are getting from their benefits.

■ *Using benefits to reinforce strategy* — the benefits package is part of total remuneration and as such can be used to send messages about organizational expectations, eg reach a certain level in the organization or achieve a certain level of performance and we will give you a better car.

■ *Cafeteria or flexible benefits* — individual employees' needs are different and it therefore makes sense to relate the benefits package to those needs by giving employees a menu of benefits to select from. One person might prefer to have school fees paid rather than receive a car. Another might prefer enhanced pension contributions. The main problem with this approach is that it is administratively and legally complex and so examples are relatively rare.

■ *Should cash be paid instead of benefits?* — it is arguable that the most flexible benefits package of all, and probably the easiest to administer, is one that just gives cash.

Activity — Pay and benefits

1. What kind of pay structure is operated in your organization?
2. On what basis is pay progression determined?
3. List the benefits that are part of your job. Try to find out just how much they are worth as a percentage of your total earnings.

References

1 Armstrong, M and Murlis, H (1991) *Reward Management*, 2nd edn, Kogan Page, London.

2 Ibid.

3 Kohn, A (1993) 'Why incentive plans cannot work', *Harvard Business Review*, September–October, pp 54–56.

4 Cushway, B and Lodge, D (1993) *Organisational Behaviour and Design*, Kogan Page, London.

5 Armstrong and Murlis, *op cit*.

6 *Remuneration and Benefits Handbook* (1994) Gee, London.

7 *Personnel Management Plus*, May 1994.

Employee Relations

This chapter is about the collective relationships between the employer and groups of staff. It refers to the formally organized vehicles for undertaking joint discussions between the two parties, ie the trade unions or staff associations and the employer, the informal relationships that are part of the process, and the mechanisms used by the organization to communicate to groups of employees. The term 'employee relations' is preferred to 'industrial relations' because the subject as covered here is wider in scope than just the system for negotiating and reaching agreement. However, much of what has been written that is of interest and relevance on this subject refers to 'industrial relations' and this is the term that will be used when describing the basis of workplace relationships.

DEFINITION AND CONTEXT OF INDUSTRIAL RELATIONS

Industrial Relations as a System

Industrial relations can be described as a system comprising:

- inputs, derived from the goals, values and power of the actors within the system;
- procedures for converting inputs into outputs;
- outputs, comprising the financial, social and psychological rewards to employees;
- a feedback loop through which outputs flow back into the industrial relations subsystem and also into the environmental subsystems.

In the first point above, goals are the objectives that the actors seek to achieve, values are the norms or standards that are observed, and power refers to the ability of an actor to satisfy his or her goals in spite of the resistance of others. The actors are the employees in their different roles as individuals, members of work teams, and trade unionists; the managers; and various other governmental or non-governmental agencies which might affect the system[1].

The procedures for converting the inputs into outputs are the mechanisms used by different organizations to arrive at conclusions that meet the goals of the various parties involved. These procedures will vary between organizations and industry sectors but will usually be some form of collective bargaining (described further below); unilateral decisions by the employer; decisions imposed by the state, the courts or some other independent body, eg where there is compulsory arbitration for certain categories of employee; or participation.

Although outputs as described above refer only to the rewards available to the employee, and arguably the main function of an industrial relations system is to allocate those rewards, the system should also seek to reward the employer, since the most desirable outcome of any negotiation is one in which both sides win. The most desirable outputs therefore are those that will also help the organization perform more effectively.

The feedback loop links the outputs from the system to the environmental subsystems. In other words, the results of the discussions and negotiations will result in changes to pay and working conditions which themselves will affect the inputs to the system. As an example, a round of high wage settlements in a number of organizations could put pressure on the general level of pay settlements in that sector. This could have further repercussions as production costs rise, possibly leading to a loss of demand, with a consequent need for the organization to make productivity savings. This situation would be even more difficult for an organization that is out of line with its competitors, having perhaps agreed a more generous settlement, or possibly even a less generous one resulting in a loss of skilled staff.

This system is shown diagramatically in Figure 9.1.

As the system of industrial relations is an open system rather than a closed one it is affected by external influences. These include the following:

- *The economy* — changes in the government's monetary and fiscal policies can affect bargaining arrangements, as for example when the public sector is restricted in the size of any pay award that can be given; employment levels can affect the bargaining power of employees, with high unemployment and relatively easy acquisition of labour strengthening the employer's position, etc.
- *Technological change* — greater mechanization and computerization can reduce the organization's need for and dependence on high numbers of staff, while at the same time requiring a different range of skills and knowledge.
- *Political decisions* — different goverments will have different economic policies and views about the balance of power in organizations.
- *The legal system* — legislation will set minimum standards or regulate the basis on which workplace relationships are conducted, as has been well demonstrated by the gradual erosion of the power of the trade unions by successive statutes in the UK over recent years.
- *Social and cultural influences* — employees and managers are part of

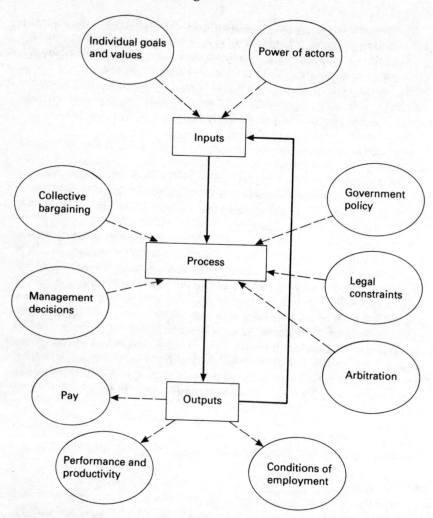

Figure 9.1 *A simplified model of the UK industrial relations system*

the wider society and will bring with them the norms and values of that society. Problems are likely to occur when the two groups have different traditions or where there is a particular constraint on the organization because of the industry sector, for example in an emergency service where there is often an expectation that the employees will not take strike action whatever the provocation.

■ *The environment* — changes in the composition or size of the population which can affect such things as demand for goods and services and availability of skilled labour, or in the climate or weather which again can affect demand in certain cases or the ability of the organization to meet its targets.

■ *Social trends* — these will affect attitudes to various aspects of industrial relations. When the miners in the UK went on strike in the 1970s, for example, they received a great deal of public support which no doubt encouraged them to hold firm. By the 1980s, however, the climate had changed and their industrial action was generally less sympathetically received. This, combined with other factors, meant that they were unsuccessful and indeed ended up with a split union.

Frames of reference

Another important feature of industrial relations is that it operates within what has been described as a pluralistic frame of reference. Whereas the opposite, the unitary frame of reference, regards the organization as having 'one source of authority and one focus of loyalty', the pluralistic view sees the organization as part of 'a plural society containing many related but separate interests and objectives which must be maintained in some kind of equilibrium'[2].

The importance of this distinction is that someone who has a unitary frame of reference will work on the assumption that the organization has a common focus and goal to which everyone will work with unswerving loyalty and dedication. This can lead to ineffective decision making. The reality is that all organizations have to satisfy several different interest groups, such as employees, managers, shareholders and customers, all with their own objectives and priorities, so the concept of one universally agreed objective does not hold much water. The basic aim of any negotiation, therefore, will not be to find the one ideal solution, but to agree on a compromise acceptable to all parties.

Industrial relations as a system of rules

Industrial relations can be regarded as a system of rules that regulate relationships in industry[3]. These rules come in many forms. They may take the form of legislation or statutory instruments, collective agreements, arbitration awards, trade union regulations, managerial decisions, social conventions, custom and practice, and so on.

The rules that regulate the employment relationship are of two types: substantive and procedural. Substantive rules refer to the detailed wages, terms and conditions contained in the agreement negotiated by the parties. Procedural rules regulate the making, interpretation and enforcement of these substantive rules, and the way in which activities are to be conducted, such as the methods to be followed for the settlement of disputes or the facilities to be accorded to shop stewards.

Collective bargaining

Collective bargaining refers to the process of negotiation between the employer and groups of employees, usually represented by one or more trade unions. One early definition is as follows:[4]

LIVERPOOL JOHN MOORES UNIVERSITY
LEARNING SERVICES

The term collective bargaining is applied to those arrangements under which wages and conditions of employment are settled by a bargain, in the form of an agreement made between employers and associations of employers and workers' organisations.

More recently, it has been defined in the Trade Union and Labour Relations (Consolidation) Act 1992 in terms of what a trade dispute might be about. In this definition, it includes negotiation about:

- terms and conditions of employment or the physical conditions in which employees are asked to work;
- engagement, non-engagement or termination or suspension of employment or dates of employment of employees;
- allocation of work or duties;
- discipline;
- membership or non-membership of a trade union;
- facilities for trade union officials;
- machinery for regulation of, or consultation on, the above matters and trade union recognition.

The pay, terms and conditions of a substantial majority of employees are settled by collective bargaining[5]. This normally takes place at one of two levels, ie nationally, in which an employer or a group of employers will negotiate and reach a national agreement affecting employees in that organization or industry, as in coal-mining and large parts of the public sector, or at local or company level where only the employees within the organization concerned will be affected. A further subdivision is plant bargaining, where only the employees at one particular site will be affected. However, bargaining can take place at more than one level and very often national negotiations will establish minimum terms which the trade unions will seek to improve at a local level. Any such local improvements can then be used as a springboard for achieving similar deals in other parts of that industry or organization.

Government intervention can also affect the agreements reached. Until recently there were a range of wages councils in the UK which established minimum wage rates. The UK goverment has also recently imposed limits on public sector pay settlements to try to keep public spending under control.

Two forms of collective bargaining have been identified. In one definition these are referred to as conjunctive bargaining and cooperative bargaining. In conjunctive bargaining the aim is to reach any agreement that is necessary to ensure that the organization, on which both parties depend, is able to continue functioning. There is in this situation an acceptance by both parties of their respective obligations and responsibilities. Cooperative bargaining recognizes the dependence of each party on the other and seeks to reach agreement based on the support of one party for the other.

Another description of these two forms of bargaining is as distributive and integrative. Distributive bargaining describes the activities involved when the aims of the two parties are in conflict, whereas integrative bargaining refers to a situation in which there is some common ground that can lead to some degree of integration of the interests of both parties.

Union recognition

Union recognition refers to an agreement by the employer to recognize a particular union or number of unions for the purposes of collective bargaining. This can involve some complicated choices, especially in a multi-union environment. Which union or unions should the organization recognize and what is the position of those employees outside the union? Recognition of one major union has the advantage of simplifying negotiations and of reducing the likelihood of demarcation disputes. However, it also gives that union more power.

This has become less of an issue in recent years with the demise of what used to be called the 'closed shop' in which an employee had to be a member of a trade union to get a job, or had to join after appointment. Such practices are now illegal. Many organizations have in fact de-recognized unions, probably a reflection of employers' strength during the past years of recession.

CURRENT ISSUES

The industrial relations scene is a constantly changing one. In the UK there has been an extensive change in recent years, from an era in which union power was seen to be a significant threat to competitiveness and when the number of days lost through strikes gained the country an unenviable reputation abroad, to the present time when union membership has fallen from some 13 million in 1979 to fewer than 10 million in 1990 and where many organizations are de-recognizing unions[6]. The whole process is about the balance of power between the employers and the employees and it is arguable that it is undesirable for either side to be considerably more powerful than the other.

Some of the main industrial relations issues at present are described below[7].

- *Individual rather than collective rights* — there has been an increasing emphasis in recent years on individual rather than collective rights, with a number of organizations which formerly had strong collective bargaining arrangements negotiating individual contracts with employees.
- *Growth of HRM* — the growth of an approach to HRM which integrates the needs of the individual and the organization is often perceived as obviating the need for a more traditional industrial relations framework.
- *More single employer bargaining* — there has been a trend away from

national or industry-wide bargaining to bargaining at the local or company level. Many of the national agreements previously made were seen as less relevant to the local needs of an organization and as giving it less control over its own destiny.

- *More decentralized bargaining* — more and more pay negotiations have been delegated to the level of the business unit, which is in line with a trend in some organizations to devolving responsibilities generally to the lowest competent level.

- *Declining union membership* — as membership declines the trade unions have to redefine their role and are likely to have to provide a wider range of services to attract new members.

- *Changes in the law relating to check-off agreements* — check-off agreements authorize the deduction by the employer of union subscriptions from pay. The law now requires individual trade union members to authorize such deductions. If the employees fail to sign any such authorization, or if the employer does not grant the facility to do so, it could have a very serious impact on union finances.

- *De-recognition* — as more unions are de-recognized, which seems to be the current inevitable trend, their influence will diminish.

- *Single union arrangements* — single union arrangements involve making agreements with one union representing all staff. Such agreements can include pendulum arbitration, in which the arbitrator has to swing one way or the other and has to award either the employer's final offer or the union's final claim, with no compromise between the two. They can also include no-strike agreements.

- *Growth of white-collar unions* — over recent years there has been a marked shift from the dominance of manual and craft unions to a much stronger presence by non-manual unions.

- *The demise of the closed shop* — pre-entry or post-entry union membership agreements, the 'closed shop' in which any new employee was required to become a member of the appropriate union to obtain or retain a particular job are now a thing of the past and this clearly has an impact on union membership.

- *Flexible working* — the need for greater flexibility in the workplace, especially in terms of multi-skilling and teamworking, and the removal of demarcation lines in jobs have led to more emphasis on flexibility bargaining. More flexibility is also required on employment conditions and working hours.

- *Harmonization* — this refers to the process of bringing all employee groups into one set of terms and conditions. Interest has grown in this because of the need to comply with legislation giving equal pay to people undertaking work that is equal in value to work undertaken by others, and because of a blurring of the differences between some manual and non-manual jobs brought about by the introduction of new technology.

- *Single-table bargaining* — this brings together unions representing both manual and non-manual workers and is regarded by many as more efficient and more likely to lead to flexible working and harmonization of pay and conditions.

PARTICIPATION

There has been a great deal of debate about employee participation or industrial democracy and a number of attempts by the European Union to develop a European policy on the subject. However, the general stance of the UK has been that such arrangements are best left to the discretion of the organization and employees concerned.

Employee participation refers to the joint involvement of both the management and the employees in making decisions that are of mutual interest. It differs from negotiation where each party has specific, different and conflicting aims that are reconciled through a process of bargaining. The term 'participation' implies more than joint consultation. In the latter, the employees will be consulted about certain courses of action by the management to ascertain their views, but it will still be for the management to make the necessary decisions. Participation aims to involve employees in the organization in such a way that their interests and those of the organization become one and the same. They should be able to achieve their own objectives by helping the organization achieve its objectives.

The main forms of employee participation are as follows:

- *Joint consultation* — this is probably the commonest form of employee participation. As stated above it involves the employer informing employees about decisions, plans and intentions to gain their views, gauge their feelings and consider suggestions. The actual process usually takes the form of a joint consultative committee, and while it may take some decisions and agree certain minor concessions, these are always within an overall framework such as that provided by a national agreement. Properly conducted they can be an effective forum for the consideration of certain issues and a means of establishing trust between the management and the employees.
- *Team briefing* — this is a means of consulting employees and of keeping them informed about decisions and actions of the organization. The aim is by briefing people in teams to build up confidence and trust and to gain commitment to the courses of action proposed.
- *Quality circles* — these go a stage further than team briefings and aim to tap into the knowledge and experience of the workforce to improve productivity and quality and gain greater commitment to the organization's objectives. They are comprised of small groups of volunteers carrying out related work who meet regularly, under a trained leader, to discuss ways of improving working methods.
- *Suggestion schemes* — suggestion schemes can be a useful way of involving employees in improving working methods and techniques.

- *Profit sharing schemes* — these can help to give employees a stake in the organization so that if the organization does well, so will they.
- *Employee communication* — employee communication in a variety of forms is important to ensure that everyone knows what the organization's aims and intentions are. Such communication takes a variety of forms, among the most common being the systematic use of the management chain, regular meetings between managers and their employees, and newsletters. Less common is the use of videos and attitude surveys.

INDUSTRIAL RELATIONS IN EUROPE[8,9]

There are wide variations in the pattern of industrial relations throughout Europe. For example, the density of union membership varies from about 75–80 per cent in Belgium and Denmark, 50 per cent in Ireland, 40 per cent in Germany and Italy and 35 per cent in Greece to as low as 10 per cent in France and Spain. However, in the case of the last two countries legally binding collective agreements cover about 80 per cent of the workforce. Union membership in the UK is at about 40 per cent.

Most European countries have some form of legal provision governing employee participation. Germany has a wide range of legal rights which include consultation on hiring and firing. In France, companies with more than 11 employees have to ensure that employee representatives are elected. In the Netherlands employers with more than 100 employees are obliged by law to establish a works council.

These differences are the inevitable result of different cultures and histories. The much vaunted German system of industry based unions, for example, was set up as part of the reconstruction of the country after World War II. However, because of the biggest economic downturn since the war, this system has lately been under pressure, to the extent that the engineering employers' federation, Gesantmetall, has for the first time cancelled existing wage, salary and holiday agreements.

There is also currently a proposal for an EU directive requiring the establishment of Europe-wide information and consultative structures, although the UK is likely to be exempt from this at least for the time being. European works councils already exist in a number of multinational companies outside the UK, although the degree of influence of the employee representatives varies. For example, while Compagnie Saint Gobain has a formal agreement for an annual conference of employee delegates, such a degree of formality is resisted by Rhône Poulenc, which nevertheless holds an annual dialogue. Allianz, a German insurance multinational, also has a company council for delegates from the European states, but has again resisted too high a degree of formality.

Further general information about employment in Europe is contained in Chapter 10.

References

1   Dunlop, J T (1958) *Industrial Relations Systems*, Holt, New York.

2   Fox, A (1966) *Industrial Sociology and Industrial Relations*, Research Paper No. 3, HMSO, London.

3   Flanders, A (1965) *Industrial Relations — What is wrong with the system?*, Faber and Faber, London.

4   *The Industrial Relations Handbook* (1964) HMSO, London.

5   Lord Donovan (1968) *Report of the Royal Commission on trades unions and employers' associations*, HMSO, London.

6   *The New Industrial Relations — Back to the Future?*, Industrial Relations Review and Report No. 559, May 1994, Eclipse Group, London.

7   Kessler, S (1993) 'Is there still a future for the unions?', *Personnel Management*, July.

8   Arkin, A (1991) 'IR in Europe: Not so distant relations', *Personnel Management*, November.

9   Tyson, S, Lawrence, P, Poirson, P, Manzolini, L and Seferi, S V (1993) *Human Resource Management in Europe — Strategic Issues and Cases*, Kogan Page, London.

10

Employment Law

This chapter sets out the main principles of employment law that any human resources manager needs to be aware of to avoid problems in the employment of people[1]. It is beyond the scope of this book to give a detailed analysis of all aspects of the law and the emphasis is rather on the essentials and the underlying principles.

The chapter examines the position at three stages of the employment process:

1. Before and on appointment.
2. During employment.
3. On termination of employment.

The UK position is reviewed first followed by a summary of practice in the rest of Europe.

BEFORE AND ON APPOINTMENT

To increase the probability of the employment relationship being a mutually satisfying and enduring one, and to ensure that it is legally sound, requires careful thought and action on the part of the employer long before the employee actually starts work. A summary of the preparatory work required to ensure that a good appointment is made is covered in Chapter 4. However, it is worth reiterating some of the points covered in that chapter, particularly to distinguish between what is essential from a legal standpoint and what is desirable. Clearly any good employer should follow what is regarded as best practice, but while failure to do so may not result in the best appointment it is unlikely to infringe any legal rules.

Any employer has to give consideration before filling a vacancy to the nature of that vacancy and indeed whether it needs to be filled at all. Assuming it does, the next step is to consider the nature of the job to be filled, taking account of present and future requirements, and from that the kind of person required. Larger organizations will usually produce a job description, setting out the requirements of the job, and a personnel specification which outlines the required attributes of the successful candidate in terms of qualifications, experience, special skills, etc. There is no legal requirement to produce a job description or a personnel specification, although it is good practice to do so.

An employer with 20 or more employees also has to employ a quota of disabled workers, ie 3 per cent of the total workforce. Also certain designated jobs, such as car park attendant, are reserved for disabled workers (Disabled Persons (Employment) Acts, 1944 and 1958).

Advertising vacancies

There are many ways of filling vacancies. These can include headhunting, advertising internally on noticeboards and through house journals, advertising in newspapers and professional journals, and recruitment by word of mouth. Which ever medium is used there are certain rules that need to be followed:

1. Any advertisement must not be discriminatory by suggesting that the job is open only to people of a particular race or sex, except in the case of what are known as 'genuine occupational qualifications' where the nature of the job calls for a man or a woman or a person of a particular race (Sex Discrimination Acts, 1975 and 1976; Race Relations Act, 1976).
2. Criteria should not be specified that are not relevant to the job but which have the effect of excluding certain categories of people, eg insisting on certain physical tests that might discriminate against women but which are not relevant to the job.
3. Avoid the use of words that have an overtly sexual connotation.
4. Bear in mind that recruitment by word of mouth or by other individual approaches could be discriminatory as it is likely to restrict applicants to a relatively limited pool.

The selection process

The employer's main concern in the selection process, apart from appointing the best candidate, should be to avoid discrimination. This means not only avoiding discrimination on grounds of race or sex, but also on grounds of trade union membership or non-membership. In effect this means not asking questions, either at interview or on the application form, which could be construed as discriminatory. A question asked of a female applicant about her marriage intentions, for example, could be construed as discriminatory against women unless all the male applicants were asked the same question. Generally such questions are best avoided.

Although there is no legal requirement to train interviewers and selection staff in the avoidance of discrimination, it is good practice to do so.

It is also unlawful for employers to take account of previous criminal offences committed by an applicant if that applicant is deemed to be rehabilitated. The rules governing this and the relevant periods of rehabilitation for various offences are set out in the Rehabilitation of Offenders Act, 1974. There are a number of jobs and professions in which such exceptions do not apply and these are set out in the Act.

Contract of employment

Having selected a suitable candidate for a job by whatever selection process, and having received satisfactory references and medical report where required, the next step is for the employer to make an offer of employment. This will normally take the form of an offer letter setting out the main terms and conditions of employment, which the candidate will either accept or negotiate on. When mutually satisfactory terms have been agreed the employer is then in a position to issue a contract of employment.

A contract of employment is very much like any other kind of contract in that there has to be:

- an offer, ie the offer of a job on certain terms and conditions;
- acceptance of that offer;
- valuable consideration, which is the employer's promise to pay wages or a salary in return for the employee's promise to work.

Although a contract can be verbal, there is a requirement in the Employ-ment Protection (Consolidation) Act, 1978, as amended by the Trade Union Reform and Employment Rights Act, 1993, for a statement of the main terms and conditions of employment to be issued to all employees (except those who work for less than eight hours a week or who are employed for less than one month) within two months of commencing their employment. In particular, employees must be issued with one document, known as the principal statement, containing key details.

Usually not all employment details can be contained in one document and the contract is really the sum of all the matters relating to the job, which might be contained in other documents such as staff handbooks or col-lective agreements. The important thing is for the employee's attention to be drawn to these other documents and for the employee to have good access to them.

DURING EMPLOYMENT

Employees' rights

Apart from any contractual obligations entered into in the contract of employment, and those arising from custom and practice in a particular organization or industry, there are a number of employees' rights that are enshrined in statute. Employees have the right:

- not to be discriminated against on grounds of race, sex, pregnancy, or membership or non-membership of a trade union;
- to a written statement of terms of employment, as referred to above;

- to an itemized statement of pay setting out the employee's gross pay and any deductions;
- to guaranteed payments that must be made to employees who are laid off because there is no work available — these payments are a limited form of compensation;
- to equal pay for the same work or for work that is equal in value (usually as assessed by some analytical method of job evaluation);
- to time off for public duties, to take part in trade union activities, duties and training and for time off to look for work if made redundant and meeting certain other criteria;
- to choose to belong to or not to belong to a trade union and to take part in trade union activities without hindrance by the employer;
- not to be unfairly dismissed (considered further below);
- to be paid redundancy payments (with the minimum level of compensation specified by statute, although employers can and usually do pay more than this level), provided certain service criteria are met;
- to protection of employment rights on the takeover of the employer's business and to redundancy pay and any arrears of pay or holiday and notice pay on the insolvency of the employer;
- not to have deductions made from wages without prior authorization;
- to statutory sick pay when absent from work through sickness for more than four days;
- to statutory maternity pay of up to 18 weeks subject to certain qualifying conditions, particularly length of service, and from October 1994, to 14 weeks' maternity leave, whether or not there is any entitlement to maternity pay;
- to certain other rights connected with maternity, including particularly the right to return to work and to suffer no detriment to terms and conditions of employment as a result of maternity absence;
- to paid leave when suspended on medical grounds to avoid breaching a particular regulation;
- to work in a safe and healthy environment;
- to 'stop the job' without suffering any penalty or detriment if the employee has good reason to suspect that the health and safety of others may be threatened;
- to be given a statutory minimum period of notice, varying with length of service and age, on being dismissed;
- to a written reason for dismissal, if requested.

The above list covers most employment rights but is not intended to be exhaustive. Some notable omissions, about which there is generally expected to be statutory rights, are hours of work and leave. Although there are some restrictions on hours of work, particularly in respect to children, shop assistants and lorry drivers, it is generally left to the employer and employee to come to whatever arrangements are mutually satisfactory. In many cases, of course, the hours of work are regulated by previously agreed collective agreements. The same applies to holidays. There is no statutory entitlement to an annual holiday and no obligation on the employer to give time off even for public holidays. It is very likely, however that most people would have a contractual entitlement to such holidays and could sue the employer for failing to provide them.

Rates of pay are generally left to be negotiated between the employer and employee. Previously in many industries rates were subject to minimum levels set by wages councils but, with the exception of the Agricultural Wages Board, these were abolished by the Trade Union Reform and Employment Rights Act, 1993.

Discipline and grievances

It is a legal requirement for any employer with 20 or more employees to make known to those employees any disciplinary rules applying to them and to give the name of any person to whom they may take any grievance. It is also strongly recommended that any employer has formal disciplinary and grievance procedures setting out clearly how such matters are to be dealt with. The absence of such procedures would substantially weaken the employer's case at an industrial tribunal.

Some of the key points to remember in dealing with any disciplinary issue are the following:

- investigate fully any disciplinary complaint before taking action;
- give the individual concerned the opportunity to respond to any complaints against him or her;
- take account of the individual's past record and performance before deciding on any disciplinary action;
- where there is an issue about performance ensure that the individual has been given all necessary training and instruction and an opportunity to improve where appropriate;
- do not dismiss for a first offence unless it is a case of gross misconduct (which is not defined);
- allow the person to be accompanied at any disciplinary hearing;
- when handling appeals ensure that a different level of management is involved from that which heard the original complaint;
- follow the organization's disciplinary procedure.

The organization should have a grievance procedure that allows grievances to be dealt with as close to their point of origin as possible.

Health and safety at work

One of the prime obligations of any employer is to provide a safe and healthy working environment. A watershed in the development of legislation to protect employees at work in the UK was the Health and Safety at Work Act, 1974. This consolidated much of the previous health and safety legislation, for the first time made infringement a criminal offence, and set up a number of new institutions, such as the Health and Safety Commission which has a key role in drawing up safety regulations and codes of practice. Although this key Act underpins UK safety legislation, a wealth of directives have emanated from the EU on these issues. Most recent EU directives are now encompassed in the following regulations (known as the 'six-pack'):

- Management of Health and Safety at Work Regulations;
- Workplace (Health, Safety and Welfare) Regulations;
- Personal Protective Equipment at Work Regulations;
- Manual Handling Operations Regulations;
- Health and Safety (Display Screen Equipment) Regulations;
- Provision and Use of Work Equipment Regulations.

Apart from the obvious requirement to comply with all relevant statutes and regulations, other key points for employers to remember on the topic of health and safety are as follows:

- Employers are required to publish a safety policy.
- The employer should nominate someone to take specific responsibility for health and safety in the organization.
- Safety representatives may be appointed by recognized independent trade unions.
- No employee should be penalized for taking action he or she considers to be necessary in the interests of health and safety.
- Adequate first-aid facilities should be provided.

TERMINATION OF EMPLOYMENT

There are a number of ways in which employment can end. These include:

- Resignation by the employee, usually with notice.
- Insolvency of the employer, in which case the employee is effectively redundant.
- Expiry of a fixed-term contract in which case employment is automatically terminated at the end of the period in question.
- Completion of a specific task in a fixed-task contract in which case employment is automatically terminated on completion of the task.
- Death of either of the parties to the contract.
- Retirement.
- By mutual agreement.
- By the contract being frustrated in some way, for example if an employee were given a term of imprisonment.
- Dismissal by the employer.

Dismissal by the employer can be for a number of reasons, which are considered below. In each case the main concern for the employer must be to ensure that any dismissal is fair, otherwise the employee might succeed in an unfair dismissal case at an industrial tribunal. Although in some cases it may be cheaper for the employer to lose an industrial tribunal case rather than retain a difficult employee, it could still involve substantial time and effort as well as being bad publicity.

Dismissal on grounds of capability or qualifications

In the case of dismissal for capability it is for the employer to prove that the employee was incapable of performing to the standard required by the employer. For such a dismissal to be effective, there must have been careful monitoring of performance, ensuring that the employee has been given all necessary training, has been told of his or her shortcomings and has also been given the opportunity to improve.

A lack of capability can also arise through ill-health and it is quite legitimate to dismiss someone for this reason. However, employers should be very careful when dealing with such cases as they are likely to be sympathetically treated by industrial tribunals. There is also a considerable difference between someone who is suffering from long-term sickness and the person who has frequent bouts of short-term sickness. The latter is very often more difficult to deal with and relies on the employer keeping accurate records of the absences. Even if the reasons are genuine it is still legitimate to dismiss someone. The main points to remember are that care needs to be exercised, the prospects of recovery carefully assessed, and the situation dealt with sympathetically.

Dismissal for a lack of appropriate qualifications is likely to be more straightforward, as the employee either has or does not have the qualifications specified. Generally this should be established at the selection stage. However, some appointments are made on condition that the successful candidate obtains a particular qualification, in which case failure to do so would render a dismissal fair. In other circumstances the employee might lose a previously held qualification, such as a driving licence. Dismissal in these circumstances would also be fair provided there were no suitable alternative employment available.

Dismissal on grounds of conduct

There are no hard and fast rules about what sort of conduct is likely to lead to dismissal. However, it is probably self-evident that certain kinds of behaviour are always going to prove unacceptable and therefore justify dismissal. These include, for example, fighting, drunkenness on duty and theft. Such misdemeanours will usually be classified as gross misconduct and justify summary dismissal, ie dismissal without notice. The seriousness with which certain behaviours are regarded, however, will vary from industry to industry and organization to organization. For this reason it is wise for any employer to have a set of disciplinary rules that are drawn to the attention of staff. In this way there is likely to be less misunderstanding about the standards of behaviour required and the rules would provide strong evidence at any tribunal hearing.

Dismissal to avoid breaching a statute

This rare example of a fair reason for dismissal arises when the continued employment of someone could lead to the employer breaching a statute. Such a situation could arise, for example, if the employer continued to employ as a driver someone who had lost his or her driving licence.

Dismissal on grounds of redundancy

This arises when a dismissal is wholly or mainly because the requirement for the kind of work carried out by the employee has ceased or diminished at that location. Where a number of employees are to be made redundant the employer is required to consult any trade unions with a view to reaching agreement about the best way to achieve the reductions planned. If more than 10 people are to be made redundant the Department of Employment also has to be notified.

Any employee made redundant has a number of rights, including:

■ the right to paid time off to look for alternative employment or arrange training;
■ the right to redundancy pay (subject to two years' service);
■ the right to notice;
■ where suitable alternative work is available (and the employer should always seek this), the right to a trial period in the new job.

Dismissal for some other substantial reason

There are range of other reasons that might make a dismissal fair. These include, for example, where a business is transferred or reorganized, where a temporary replacement for a woman on maternity leave is dismissed, or where it might be necessary for the protection of the organization, eg where an employee refuses to accept a non-competition clause in a contract.

Constructive dismissal

This is not, strictly speaking, a form of dismissal, but rather occurs when the employee resigns because of what he or she considers to be unreasonable behaviour on the part of the employer. For such a case to be successful at an industrial tribunal, the behaviour complained of would need to go to the root of the employment contract. A demotion without good cause might be such a reason.

EMPLOYMENT PRACTICE IN EUROPE[2]

Some of the main features of employment practice in Europe are summarized in Table 10.1.

Table 10.1 *Employment conditions in Europe*

Country	Pay	Hours	Holidays	Maternity rights	Industrial relations	Employment protection
France	National minimum wage. Participation in profit related pay scheme is compulsory for companies with more than 50 employees.	Legal maximum of 39 hours per week. Above this overtime is payable but this must not exceed an average of 46 hours over 12 weeks or 48 in one week. An employee must not work for 6 days in a row without a break of at least 24 hours.	2.5 days per month worked.	16 weeks' leave for first two children and 26 weeks for others. 84% of daily wage free of tax and social security. Pregnant employees cannot be sacked.	Collective agreements have the force of law. There are a number of employer/ employee committees with various functions with the trade unions siting on all of them.	It is unlawful to seek references by telephone or in writing. When an employee leaves the employer must provide a work certificate which must not make any reference to the employee's performance.
Belgium	National minimum wage in sectors where there is no collective agreement. Gross pay is adjusted twice a year in line with the retail prices index. This may not be replaced by bonuses or other payments.	Legal maximum of 40 hours. It is illegal to work on Sundays except where provided by law.	20 working days after one year's employment. Actual agreements more generous.	15 weeks' maternity leave, at least 8 of which must be taken after the birth.	Collective agreements at sector and national level are legally binding, as are company deals if published.	
Germany	No statutory minimum wage but collective agreements are binding.	Legal maximum of 48 hours but most collective agreements stipulate 37–40 hours.	Statutory minimum of 18 days but most agreements provide for longer.	Statutory maternity leave of 14 weeks, 6 weeks to be taken before the birth and 8 weeks after.	Two-tier structure with a supervisory board that appoints an executive board. Highly regulated with employers having to consult on a range of issues. Industry-wide unions so few demarcation disputes.	Must be a socially justifiable reason for any dismissal, except on grounds of behaviour.

Table 10.1   *Employment conditions in Europe* (contd)

Country	Pay	Hours	Holidays	Maternity rights	Industrial relations	Employment protection
Netherlands	Minimum wage for all employees who work more than one-third of normal hours.	Legal maximum of 8 per day or 40 per week. Saturday and Sunday working prohibited unless nature of business makes it necessary.	15 days per annum, but after one year's service at least 4 times the number of working days in the week. Must be given paid leave for marriage (2 days), bereavement (4 days) and other family obligations (1 day).	16 weeks, 4 to be taken before birth. Benefit equal to normal wage. Parents with one year's service and children under 4 entitled to work shorter hours for 6 months.	Collective agreements are legally binding. Companies with over 35 employees must establish a works council elected by employees which must meet 6 times a year and consent to certain major issues.	Probationary periods are common but must not last for more than 2 months. After this the employee must be retained. Dismissal can only be with permission from regional labour office.
Italy	Minimum pay levels established by collective agreements.	Legal maximum of 8 hours per day and 48 per week. Most work 40 hours with national contracts limiting overtime.	10 national public holidays plus local holidays. Annual holiday entitlement set out in national agreements.	2 months before expected date of birth, 3 months after, with further 6 months optional. Employment protected during pregnancy and year after birth.	Constitution gives right to unions to negotiate contracts binding on all those within the scope of the agreement.	
Denmark	No statutory minimum wage but collective agreements state minimal or normal rates.	37 hours, nationally agreed.	Holiday entitlement laid down as 2.5 days per month.	4 weeks' paid leave before birth, 24 weeks after, 10 of which may be taken by either parent.	Over 80% union membership. Companies with over 35 employees may set up cooperation committees elected by the workforce.	
Greece	Minimum salaries for different employee categories. All employees get the equivalent of 14 monthly salaries in a year.	Shift from 6 to 5 day week in last decade. Standard working hours are 40 per week.	20 working days increasing to 22 after each year of continuous service for those working 5-day week. 12 public holidays.	15 weeks, 52 days to be taken before and 53 after the birth. Mother given one hour's paid leave each day for one year after.	Labour law not clearly defined. Industrial relations has legacy of mistrust.	Some protection for mothers and trade unions and legislation against mass dismissal — usually 2% of workforce.

References

[1]   *Essential Facts — Employment* (1994) Gee & Co, London.

[2]   Brewser, C, Hegewisch, A, Holden, L and Lockhart, T (1992) *The European Human Resource Management Guide*, Academic Press, London.

11

Employment Procedures

This chapter focuses on an number of miscellaneous procedures that are an essential part of effective human resource management but which will do not fall obviously under any of the previous chapter headings. They are processes that are either a legal requirement or are necessary for effective day-to-day management of people. The procedures considered are:

- personnel records;
- timekeeping and absence;
- redundancy;
- relocation;
- equal opportunities;
- policies on smoking, drinking, harassment, etc.

PERSONNEL RECORDS

Any organization has to keep detailed records on its employees[1]. Not only are many of these a legal requirement, such as the contract of employment and pay and benefits information, but they are also essential for effective human resource management. Without such records managers will find it difficult, if not impossible, to plan future staffing requirements, develop cost-effective training programmes or manage performance.

The fundamental records required are:

- personal details of the employee;
- the employee's employment history;
- details of the job including job title, department, location, grade, etc.
- terms and conditions attaching to the job;
- the employee's absence record;
- the employee's disciplinary record;
- any training given to the employee;
- any performance appraisal information;
- job evaluation data.

The organization should have sufficient information held in such a form that it can analyse employees by age, length of service, grade or pay rate, and sex. Information should also be kept on ethnic origin, or whether the employee is registered disabled. It should be possible to provide summary data about labour turnover and retention rates, absence, timekeeping, salary and wage costs, and accidents.

The information should be sufficient for the organization to undertake ethnic monitoring so that managers can be sure that equal opportunities policies are working effectively.

Personnel records may be kept in many different forms, from card index systems to computers. The actual system used will naturally depend on the number of employees involved. However, where personnel data is held on computer the employer must be sure to conform to the provisions of the Data Protection Act, 1984.

Using a CPIS

A computerized personnel information system (CPIS) can take a lot of the drudgery out of maintaining personnel records, will give faster access to data and can be used for modelling and human resource planning (see Table 11.1)[2]. By integrating such systems with the payroll detailed cost forecasts can be made. Similarly, the use of networking can give several geographically remote sites access to information, thus reducing the amount of written or telephone communication necessary with the centre and reinforcing a corporate approach. Electronic mail also provides a swift and accessible communication medium. Many multimedia systems now in use can include personal details and photographs of thousands of individual employees.

Whitbread Inns, which is responsible for 1600 public houses and 22,000 staff, has an incentive bonus scheme known as the 'Share-inn success scheme' which awards points to pub teams based on sales and hours of

Table 11.1 *Uses of a CPIS*

Personnel records
Recruitment and selection
Organization charts
Controlling absence
Monitoring equal opportunities
Performance appraisal and potential assessment
Succession planning
Training and development planning and control
Screen based testing
Accident records
HR planning and budgeting
Labour turnover, wastage and retention rates
Productivity measures
Compensation strategy design
Communication

---

work. The data on which judgements are made are obtained from a videotext based system that captures weekly payroll and business figures, data from the general ledger and payroll system, and sales data from each inn via an electronic point of sale system. This information is integrated with data from the personnel information system to produce targets for product drives and sales[3].

Activity — information management

Review how information is managed in your organization.

1. Is there a CPIS?
2. What is this used for?
3. Is any use made of E-mail (electronic mail)?
4. How reliable is management and personnel information?

TIMEKEEPING AND ABSENCE

Absence is a significant problem, estimated to cost the UK alone a huge £13 billion a year. Studies carried out over recent years have shown the UK's absence rates to be considerably higher than those in the rest of Europe — a 1983 study showed Britain's absence rate at 11.8 per cent compared with 5.9 per cent for France, 5.4 per cent for the Netherlands, 3.8 per cent for Belgium, 3 per cent for West Germany and Sweden and 2.9 per cent for Italy[4]. More recent studies appear to indicate that the position has not changed substantially[5]. Assuming all statistics were compiled with equal rigour, it is clearly very important for Britain in particular to try to keep absence under control and to reduce it wherever possible.

Absence, in this context, refers to a situation in which a person who is scheduled for work does not turn up at the expected time, for whatever reason. While the given reason may be sickness, there could be numerous underlying causes which the employer needs to be aware of. For example, absence can be affected by:

■ working conditions;
■ working relationships;
■ induction or training received;
■ health and safety;
■ job content;
■ quality of management;
■ disciplinary standards;
■ individual motivation and commitment;
■ domestic circumstances;
■ stress.

The first stage in the absence management process is ensuring that there is accurate information available at both the individual and the organizational level so that the problem can be monitored and managed.

The information that needs to be maintained includes[6]:

- number of days' absence at individual, section and department level;
- numbers of spells of absence at individual, section and department level;
- reasons for absences;
- whether absences are certificated or uncertificated;
- employee details;
- costs of absence.

The information should be thorough enough to enable the employer to identify patterns of absence, such as a high incidence of sickness at bank holidays.

There also need to be clear procedures for managing absence. These should include the following:

- Clear written guidelines for employees on reporting absences.
- Clear written guidelines and training for managers on handling absences.
- Making managers take responsibility for absence rather than leaving it to the personnel department.
- Involving employee representatives in the monitoring process.
- Ensuring that senior staff set an example.
- Setting (unpublished) targets for absence levels.
- Computerizing absence records incorporating trigger mechanisms to highlight absences above a certain level.
- Conducting return to work interviews.
- Identifying likely poor attenders before selection.

A number of these approaches have been found helpful in reducing absence. Computerized absence management programs are available with the built-in trigger mechanisms referred to. The Swedish-owned company SCA Packaging has long used employee representatives in its UK operation to assist with absence monitoring and they are, if anything, rather tougher on absence control than management. Iveco Ford Truck has managed to reduce absence by almost half through a similar approach which has demonstrated the power of peer group pressure[7].

Some organizations use financial incentives such as attendance bonuses, or disincentives such as not permitting overtime to be earned until a certain level of attendance has been achieved. Peugeot, for example, pays a weekly bonus for full attendance over the previous four weeks. Similarly, Toshiba pays a lump sum for full attendance. However, there is no firm evidence that these actually improve attendance and their use may be more symbolic in nature.

There are also a number of strategic approaches that can be used to reduce absence levels. These are aimed rather more at tackling the underlying causes of absence. They include:

- Promoting a healthy lifestyle.

- Ensuring a safe and healthy environment.
- Promoting flexible patterns of working.
- Improving working conditions.
- Providing an occupational health and welfare service.
- Job enrichment.
- Developing a performance culture.

Of all the suggested approaches, arguably the most important is encouraging an environment where the focus is on performance and results. Regular attendance is important, but high productivity and quality outputs are also required and attendance alone does not guarantee their attainment.

REDUNDANCY

While there is a statutory minimum level of compensation that has to be paid to anyone made redundant, the organization should also have its own redundancy and severance policy. This might include compensation above the statutory minima as well as provision for outplacement counselling.

The organization should plan ahead to try to avoid redundancies but prepare a procedure to handle them should they prove necessary. When seeking staff reductions the organization should first call for volunteers. If these are insufficient in number other actions may have to be considered.

Before implementing any redundancies the organization should consider alternative ways of reducing staff costs. These might include:

- cancelling any subcontracted labour;
- removing overtime;
- trying to obtain additional work or orders;
- dismissing part-time staff;
- job sharing;
- reducing hours.

It is in the interests of the organization to provide a comprehensive severance and outplacement service, as this will reduce the likelihood of any recriminations from those leaving and sends positive messages to remaining staff, whose morale might otherwise suffer. It also enhances the organization's image with the public at large.

RELOCATION

The organization might require staff to relocate to a different part of the country from time to time, perhaps because of a reorganization, because of increased accommodation costs or because it has outgrown existing premises. In such circumstances it should be particularly careful about dealing with employees and their representatives, bearing in mind that their willingness to move will be strongly affected by their domestic circumstances.

Full information should be given to employees about the area the organization is considering moving to and a comprehensive relocation package should be offered. This will be likely to include such things as:

- reimbursement of all costs associated with moving house, such as legal and estate agent's fees, survey fees, insurance and removal costs;
- reimbursement of indirect costs such as new carpets and curtains or telephone installation;
- assistance with arranging a mortgage;
- payment of any excess housing costs;
- payment of a disturbance allowance;
- reimbursement of any house-hunting costs.

In some cases it may be worthwhile to engage a relocation agency to assist.

EQUAL OPPORTUNITIES

The legal position on sex and race discrimination is considered in more detail in Chapter 10. The organization should have in place processes and procedures to ensure that it does not discriminate on the grounds of:

- sex;
- maternity;
- disability;
- race.

Any discrimination on these grounds is illegal. It could also be argued that there should not be any discrimination on the grounds of age, and in some countries, such as France, this is a legal requirement. However, it is not a legal restriction in the UK although discrimination on this basis will be likely to exclude talented and experienced people.

The organization should develop an equal opportunities policy and ensure its effectiveness by:

- making a senior manager responsible for the policy;
- agreeing the contents with employee representatives where necessary;
- providing training in the policy for supervisors and others;
- making all staff and job applicants aware of the policy;
- regularly monitoring the policy.

Potential sex discrimination can be monitored by analysing whether members of one sex:

- apply for jobs or promotion in smaller numbers than might be expected;
- are recruited, promoted or trained in a lower proportion than their rate of application;
- are concentrated in certain jobs or departments.

Ethnic monitoring to avoid potential race discrimination should review:

■ the number and relative proportions of employees by racial group;
■ the distribution of these employees by skill and job grade;
■ induction programmes and training needs;
■ the policy and procedures for promotion.

POLICIES ON SMOKING AND SUBSTANCE ABUSE

Miscellaneous policies might exist on such issues as smoking and substance abuse. A smoking policy seeks to provide a healthy working environment and to avoid friction between smokers and non-smokers. Probably the most common arrangement is to ban smoking in all areas except those specially designated for the purpose.

Substance abuse relates to the use of alcohol, drugs or other substances in a way that reduces working efficiency and produces disciplinary problems. It is as well for the employer to have a policy on such matters as this kind of abuse has become increasingly common and if not controlled could result in considerable disruption. It is also an absolute obligation on the employer to provide a safe working environment and curbs therefore need to be placed on such abuse in the workplace.

HARASSMENT

The Institute of Personnel and Development has recently produced a statement on harassment at work,[8] which is a subject that is now receiving greater attention. As the IPD points out, there is no simple definition of harassment as it may take a number of different forms, such as unwelcome physical contact, jokes and gossip, graffiti, gestures, isolation, coercion or pestering. It can cause considerable distress to the person affected, both at work and at home. It can result in reduced morale, greater absenteeism, lower efficiency and divided teams. To counter harassment the IPD recommends the following:

■ A published and well-promoted policy statement supported by top management.
■ Clear, fair and user-friendly procedures to resolve problems quickly and confidentially.
■ Access to counselling and support.
■ Thorough and immediate investigation of any allegations.
■ Swift, sensitive and effective remedies.
■ Use of grievance and disciplinary procedures where appropriate.
■ Protection of confidentiality as far as possible.
■ A sustained programme of communication, monitoring and training.

Activity — Policies and procedures

Review one of your organization's personnel policies. Is it:

- clear;
- understandable;
- communicated to all employees;
- implemented in practice;
- supported by management;
- supported by staff and unions;
- effective;
- fair;
- regularly reviewed?

References

[1] *Employment Handbook* (1990) Advisory, Conciliation and Arbitration Service, London.

[2] Evans, A (1991) *Computers and Personnel Systems*, IPM, London.

[3] Richards-Carpenter, C (1992) 'Systems which set the pace', *Personnel Management*, November.

[4] Huczynski, A and Fitzpatrick, M (1990) 'Absenteeism', *Personnel Management Factsheet*, April.

[5] Emslie, A (1993) 'Sickness as a business issue', *Journal of Employment Law and Practice*, Vol 1, No 1.

[6] Cushway, B (1993) 'How to improve attendance at work', *Journal of Employment Law and Practice*, Vol 1, No 1.

[7] Arkin, A (1993) 'The workforce who got sick of absenteeism', *Personnel Management Plus*, November.

[8] *Statement on harassment at work* (1994) Institute of Personnel and Development, Wimbledon.

Glossary

Action learning   an approach developed by Revans which is based on the principle that people learn best by doing and by the consideration of real problems in real environments.

Assessment centre   a planned programme of tests, exercises and group selection techniques designed to assess the suitability of participants for promotion in general or for a particular job.

Behavioural event interview   a variant of the critical incident method (see below) used to gain information about the competencies relevant to a job by obtaining detailed narrative accounts of how both superior and average performers thought and acted during critical incidents in their jobs, including successes and failures.

Bio data   biographical information including age, qualifications and jobs, usually used for selection purposes.

Case study   a short history or description, often based on a real event, which is used to teach trainees how to diagnose and resolve problems in that context.

Check-off agreements   authorization of the deduction of union subscriptions by the employer from pay. The law requires individual trade union members to authorize such deductions.

Coaching   a method of training in which the trainee is given general support and guidance with the emphasis more on helping the individual teach himself or herself and on ensuring that he or she acquires the necessary knowledge, skills and experience to undertake a job to the required standard. The term is also used to describe a management style in which the emphasis is on the manager providing such support and guidance to staff.

Cohort or survival analysis   an analysis of how long a particular group remains within the organization.

Collective bargaining   the process of negotiation between the employer and groups of employees, usually represented by one or more trade unions.

Competency   an underlying characteristic of an individual which is causally related to effective or superior performance in a job.

Critical incident method   a means of obtaining information about a job by asking the person doing it to recall incidents critical to the performance of different aspects of the job and how these were dealt with.

Decision banding   a method of evaluating jobs according to the level and types of decisions made.

Demonstration   a means of training someone to do a job by showing him or her how to do it, sometimes described as 'sitting next to Nellie'.

Development   the process of giving individuals the necessary knowledge, skills and experience to enable them to be able to undertake greater and more demanding roles and responsibilities.

Development centre   a variant of the assessment centre (see above) in which a whole battery of tests, such as psychometric assessment, group discussions and in-tray exercises, are used on a group of people to assess their skills, competencies or knowledge, and therefore their suitability for certain roles.

Do-it-yourself training   an approach to training based on the assumption that people learn most effectively when they have to find things out for themselves, subject to overall guidelines.

Factor comparison   a method of job evaluation in which jobs are compared with each other on a number of different factors rather than as whole jobs. This produces a number of different hierarchies of jobs as some will be high on some factors but low on others. Comparisons are then made of the lists of factor rankings and judgements made about how much of each job is attributable to the various factors.

Graded salary structure   a number of pay ranges or grades each with a specified maximum and minimum and through which an individual postholder will progress on the basis of experience, performance or length of service. Jobs are allocated to grades according to their size with broadly comparable jobs being placed within the same grade.

Graphology   the analysis of personality from an individual's handwriting, usually for selection purposes.

Group dynamics   a range of techniques designed to improve group effectiveness, based on behavioural science research.

Half-life index   time taken for half a homogeneous group within the organization to leave through natural wastage.

Harassment   there is no simple definition of harassment as it may take a number of different forms, such as unwelcome physical contact, jokes and gossip, graffiti, gestures, isolation, coercion or pestering.

Harmonization   the process of bringing all employee groups into one set of terms and conditions.

Hierarchical task analysis   a method of job analysis in which jobs are broken down into a hierarchical set of tasks, which are in turn broken down into sub-tasks. They are defined in terms of their objectives or outputs and also the way in which these are to be achieved. The process entails describing what needs to be done, the standards to which it has to be done, and any conditions associated with task performance.

Human resource management (HRM)   a range of strategies, processes and activities designed to support corporate objectives by integrating the needs of the organization and the individuals that comprise it.

Human resource planning   the systematic and continuing process of analysing an organization's human resource needs under changing conditions and developing personnel policies appropriate to longer-term effectiveness. It is an integral part of corporate planning and budgeting procedures since human resource costs and forecasts both affect and are affected by longer-term corporate plans.

Job analysis   a process used to determine and describe the content of jobs in such a way that a clear understanding of what the job is about is communicated to anyone who might require the information for management purposes.

Job classification   a method of job evaluation (see below) which identifies a number of classes or grades of employee, each of which will have certain characteristics and into which all jobs with these characteristics can be placed.

Job description   a written statement of the content of any particular job derived from the analysis of that job.

Job evaluation   a process for judging the relative size or importance of jobs within an organization.

Job family   a group of jobs of similar type usually identified for job evaluation, pay or career progression purposes.

Job rotation   training by moving employees into other jobs for a period to enable them to acquire new and wider skills and to gain a wider appreciation of those other jobs.

Joint consultation   probably the commonest form of employee participation, it involves the employer informing employees about decisions, plans and intentions to gain their views, gauge their feelings and consider suggestions.

National vocational qualifications (NVQs)   an attempt in the UK to rationalize the numerous different types and levels of qualifications in one national standard with several different levels of attainment.

Organization development (OD)   a range of strategies, techniques and approaches, based on behavioural science research, aimed at individuals, groups, teams and the whole organization and designed to change the culture of that organization.

Outdoor development   an approach to training in which trainees are sent on courses which include a significant degree of outdoor physical activity such as rockclimbing or canoeing, based on the assumption that such training is likely to be character forming.

Paired comparisons   a method of job evaluation similar to ranking (see below) in that complete jobs are compared with all other jobs and scores are allocated in terms of whether a particular job is as important, more important or less important than another. In this way, by giving points to each job in turn on the basis of these comparisons, a rank order may be produced.

Participant observation   a means of obtaining information about a job by actually doing it.

Participation   the joint involvement of both the management and the employees of the organization in making decisions that are of mutual interest.

Pay or progression curves   pay rates applied to different levels of competence and depending on prevailing market rates, usually applied to professional jobs.

Pay spine   a series of incremental points extending from the smallest job to the largest, usually then divided into grades.

Performance management   a process designed to manage employees' performance in such a way that their individual objectives and those of the organization can both be met, as far as possible.

Performance related pay (PRP)   any system of payment that is related to the attainment of some performance objective.

Personnel management   a series of activities which enable working people and their employing organizations to agree about the objectives and nature of their working relationship, and ensure that the agreement is fulfilled.

Personnel specification   whereas the job description describes the content of a particular job, the personnel or person specification describes the attributes required of an employee to carry out the job described to a satisfactory standard.

Points rating   a method of job evaluation which consists of the identification of a number of factors considered to be relevant to all the jobs under consideration with points allocated to the different levels of these factors. Jobs are compared against each of these factors, and points allocated accordingly, and then the separate factors are totalled to give an overall score.

Procedural agreement   a term used in industrial relations to describe an agreement about the procedures governing the conduct of employer/employee relations in an organization, eg on how to deal with a collective bargaining dispute.

Quality circles   these aim to tap into the knowledge and experience of the workforce to improve productivity and quality and gain greater commitment to the organization's objectives. They are comprised of small groups of volunteers carrying out related work who meet regularly, under a trained leader, to discuss ways of improving working methods.

Ranking   a means of evaluating whole jobs by comparing each job with every other job and placing them in order of importance to the organization.

Red-circling   a term used to describe the process by which jobs that have been downgraded following a job evaluation exercise are protected at their existing salary level until such time that they are vacated by the present incumbent.

Repertory grid   a job analysis technique which focuses on job content by differentiating between good and poor performers based on obtaining personal constructs, which are individuals' views about the world.

Retention profile   the percentages of different groups of staff remaining with the organization expressed as a proportion of new entrants.

Role playing   a training technique in which individuals consider a problem or situation in much the same way as a case study (see above) except that each plays a different role in the case being considered.

Single-table bargaining a process which brings together unions representing both manual and non-manual workers, regarded by many as more efficient and more likely to lead to flexible working and harmonization of pay and conditions.

Spot rate a single pay figure for a particular job.

Stability index a measurement of the number of staff tending to remain with the organization.

Staff turnover the number of staff leaving in any one year, usually expressed as a percentage of the average number of staff employed during that year.

Substantive agreement a term used in industrial relations to describe any agreement relating to pay or conditions of employment, as distinct from procedures.

Team briefing a means of consulting employees and of keeping them informed about decisions and actions of the organization. The aim is, by briefing people in teams, to build up confidence and trust and to gain commitment to the courses of action proposed.

Technology based training (TBT) any desk based technique which enables the individual to work through a training programme using interactive computer programs, videos or compact discs.

Timespan of discretion a method of evaluating jobs according to the timescale over which the individual has the discretion to make decisions.

Training a planned process to modify attitude, knowledge or skill behaviour through learning experience to achieve effective performance in an activity or range of activities. Its purpose, in the work situation, is to develop the abilities of the individual and to satisfy the current and future staffing needs of the organization.

Training gap the difference between a person's actual performance in a job and the desired performance, which can be bridged by training.

Union membership agreements 'closed shop' agreements which required any new employee to become a member of the appropriate union to get or retain a particular job. They have now been abolished.

Union recognition an agreement by the employer to recognize a particular union or number of unions for the purposes of collective bargaining (see above).

Bibliography

ACAS (1984) *Recruitment and Selection*, Advisory Booklet No 6, London.

ACAS (1990) *Employment Handbook*, London.

Armstrong, M (1991) *A Handbook of Personnel Management Practice*, 4th edn, Kogan Page, London.

Armstrong, M and Murlis, H (1991) *Reward Management: A Handbook of Remuneration Strategy and Practice*, Kogan Page, London.

Barrick, M R and Mount, M K (1991) 'The big five personality dimensions and job performance: a meta-analysis', *Personnel Psychology*, 44.

Boyatzis, R E (1982) *The Competent Manager: A Model for Effective Performance*, Wiley-Interscience, New York.

Bridgford, J and Stirling, J (1994) *Employee Relations in Europe*, Blackwell, Oxford.

Cushway, B (ed) (1994) *Essential Facts — Employment*, Gee & Co, London.

Cushway, B and Lodge, D (1993) *Organisational Behaviour and Design*, Kogan Page, London.

Evans, A (1991) *Computers and Personnel Systems*, IPM, London.

Hamblin, A C (1974) *Evaluation and Control of Training*, McGraw-Hill, Maidenhead.

HR-BC Ltd and Industrial Relations Services (1993) *Competency and the Link to HR Practice — A Survey of Leading Organisations*.

Incomes Data Services Ltd (1993) *Management Bonus Schemes*, Research File 28, November.

Jaques, E (1961) *Equitable Payment*, Heinemann, Oxford.

Lee, G and Beard, D (1994) *Development Centres*, McGraw Hill, Maidenhead.

Lockett, J (1992) *Effective Performance Management*, Kogan Page, London.

Manpower Services Commission (1981) *Glossary of Training Terms*, 3rd edn, HMSO, London.

McBeath, G (1992) *The Handbook of Human Resource Planning — Practical Manpower Analysis Techniques for HR Professionals*, Blackwell, Oxford.

McCormick, E J, Jeanneret, P R and Mecham, R C (1972) 'A study of job characteristics and job dimensions based on the Position Analysis Questionnaire (PAQ)', *Journal of Applied Psychology*, vol 56.

Megginson, D, Joy-Matthews, J and Banfield, P (1993) *Human Resource Development*, Kogan Page, London.

Mitrani, A, Dalziel, M and Fitt, D (eds) (1992) *Competency Based Human Resource Management: Value-driven Strategies for Recruitment, Development and Reward*, Kogan Page, London.

Neale, F (ed) (1991) *Handbook of Performance Management*, IPM, London.

Pearn, M and Kandola, R (1988) *Job Analysis — A Practical Guide for Managers*, IPM, London.

Pedler, M (ed) (1991) *Action Learning in Practice*, Gower, Aldershot.

Peters, T and Austin, N (1986) *A Passion for Excellence: The Leadership Difference*, Fontana, London.

Porter, M (1985) *Competitive Advantage*, Collier Macmillan, New York.

Pritchard, D and Murlis, H (1992) *Jobs, Roles and People*, Nicholas Brealey Publishing, London.

Revans, R (1983) *The ABC of Action Learning*, Chartwell Bratt, Bromley.

Schmitt, N, Gooding, R Z, Noe, R A and Kirsch, M (1984) 'Meta-analysis of validity studies published between 1964 and 1982 and the investigation of study characteristics', *Personnel Psychology*, 37.

Smith, M (ed) (1991) *Analysing Organizational Behaviour*, Macmillan, London.

Spencer, Lyle M Jr, McClelland, D C and Spencer, S M (1992) *Competency Assessment Methods: History and State of the Art*, Hay/McBer Research Press.

Torrington, D and Hall, L (1991) *Personnel Management — A New Approach*, 2nd edn, Prentice Hall, London.

Tyson, S, Lawrence, P, Poirson, P, Manzolini, L and Seferi, S V (1993) *Human Resource Management in Europe — Strategic Issues and Cases*, Kogan Page, London.

Index